MICROWAVE
CRAFT
MAGIC

MICROWAVE CRAFT MAGIC

MARJIE LAMBERT

JG PRESS

DEDICATION
To my sister Susie, whose creativity has always been an inspiration

A QUINTET BOOK

Published in the USA 1996 by JG Press.
Distributed by World Publications, Inc.

The JG Press imprint is a trademark of
JG Press, Inc.
455 Somerset Avenue
North Dighton, MA 02764

This edition produced for sale in the USA, its territories and dependencies only.

ISBN 1-57215-178-1

This book was designed and produced by
Quintet Publishing Limited
6 Blundell Street
London N7 9BH

Project Editor: Laura Sandelson
Creative Director: Richard Dewing
Designers: Pete Laws, Chris Dymond
Editor: Beverly LeBlanc
Photographer: Nelson Hargreaves

Typeset in Great Britain by
Central Southern Typesetters, Eastbourne
Manufactured in Hong Kong by
Regent Publishing Services Limited
Printed in Singapore by
Star Standard Industries (Pte) Ltd

AUTHOR'S ACKNOWLEDGEMENTS
Special thanks to Terry, who cheered me on and cleaned up my messes; to Laura at Quintet for her guidance; and to Vicki and Clare for their support.

WARNING

Every effort has been made to ensure that all information in this book is accurate. However due to differing conditions, microwave ovens and individual skills, neither the author nor Quintet Publishing Limited warrant or guarantee any of the projects or formulae contained herein nor do they assume any liability for any injuries, losses, or other damage that might result to readers and/or their microwave ovens or utensils. Nor can the author or Quintet Publishing Limited assume any liability for any damages that may occur as a result of reading and following the projects in this book. The purchase of this book by the reader will serve as an acknowledgement of these disclaimers.

CONTENTS

introduction

ABOVE Straw-flowers are ideal candidates for microwave drying, are available in numerous shades, and, therefore, are often the foundation of dried flower designs.

In the 1970s, when the microwave oven began to emerge as a useful and affordable kitchen tool, many regarded it with suspicion. The claims of easy, quick meals seemed too good to be true, and the technology was unfamiliar, like a strange and potentially threatening magical force. But slowly the boldest of our friends and neighbors were won over. When we saw their successes and the safety of the technology, we cautiously tried boiling water and thawing muffins in the microwave ovens, then followed increasingly sophisticated recipes until we too became converts. Today, for many cooks, the microwave oven is an important tool, as essential as an electric mixer or a wooden spoon.

Now, with the microwave oven such a standard fixture in most kitchens, it can be used for much more than just food preparation. It is also an invaluable tool for craft hobbyists, radically cutting the time required for many processes like flower drying and ornament making. These quicker times make experimentation and creativity much easier, and mistakes much less frustrating, because it no longer takes a week, for example, to dry a small bunch of flowers to replace any ruined blossoms.

Anyone like myself who cherishes the intimacy of giving homemade gifts can expand their repertoire beyond the traditional cookies and preserves. Sweet-scented potpourri, lovely dried flower arrangements, whimsical dough and papier-mâché items, and even beauty products, all become so much easier by using the microwave oven.

This book contains step-by-step instructions for more than 70 projects that use the microwave. You can follow these "recipes," or use them to inspire your own creations.

First, however, you must understand how the microwave works. The "magic" begins with a magnetron tube that emits extremely short, high-frequency electromagnetic waves called microwaves. Aided by a spinning propeller, the microwaves enter the oven, bounce off the walls, and concentrate on whatever is in the oven – a cup of water, a bowl of broccoli, or a platter of rose petals to be dried for potpourri.

The items are not cooked solely by the microwaves, but also by the conduction of heat that spreads inward from the point where each microwave penetrates the surface. The microwaves penetrate an inch or so into the surface of the item, causing molecules of sugar, fat, water, or

It is critical to experiment with your microwave.

This is because in microwave ovens, more so than in conventional ovens, the size, density, quantity, and uniformity of the items being cooked can cause cooking times to vary dramatically. Small pieces cook considerably faster than large ones. Light, porous items like rose petals take less time than dense items like dough ornaments. Four items take approximately twice as long to bake as two items.

In food preparation, most microwave cooking is done on the high setting, or 100 percent power. Many of the items in this book are small or delicate substances that dry rapidly. Consequently, I recommend cooking them longer at lower settings. At high power, you have a margin of error of only a few seconds before your creations are ruined. The microwave oven is more forgiving at lower settings.

other substances to vibrate. The microwaves quickly run out of energy, but the vibrations cause friction, which in turn creates heat. The heat spreads through the food, cooking it. The same process that cooks food applies whether you're heating sweet almond oil for a moisturizer, silica gel to dry flowers, or a dough Christmas ornament.

The effect of microwaves can be seen in the drying of a flat dough ornament. Because the ornament is thin, the microwaves that bounce at it from all directions overlap in the middle, cooking the middle faster and potentially causing it to scorch.

ABOVE *All the flowers in this Gypsy Basket have been dried in the microwave – an invaluable tool for craft hobbyists, radically cutting the time required for many processes like flower drying and ornament making.*

When you turn off the oven's power, the microwaves stop, but the molecules continue to vibrate, spreading heat and therefore the item continues cooking for a few minutes. I find it wise to slightly undercook items, then leave them to stand for five to 10 minutes.

EXPERIMENTING WITH YOUR MICROWAVE

Experimentation with times and power levels is critical when using microwaves. Not only might you need to adjust the cooking times or power levels to suit your own microwave, but many other factors affect cooking in a microwave. The projects in this book were tested on a 700-watt microwave oven. Thus instructions that call for 50 percent power use 350 watts, while recipes that call for 30 percent power need 210 watts. Use those levels only as guidelines however. I cannot stress enough, experiment with your torn blossoms and your lopsided Christmas ornaments, until you have a sense of how quickly your oven accomplishes each task.

LEFT The cardinal rule about containers and the microwave is that metal should never be used. Materials that are considered microwave-safe are: tempered glass, clay or ceramics; microwave-safe plastic or rubber; or cardboard.

Some cooks, for example, like taking 45 minutes at a medium-low setting to cook a dark roux, while others prefer to do it in 10 minutes over extremely high heat. Also, dense items like dough cook more evenly at low settings. As you become more comfortable with making crafts in the microwave, adjust the cooking times and settings to suit your own style.

The optimum way to cook in a microwave is to group items of uniform size and shape together, then arrange them around the edge of a microwave-safe platter on top of a carousel or turntable. If that isn't possible, arrange the largest, densest items at the outside, where they cook faster. You may need to periodically shift items from the center to the outside for even cooking, just as you would switch two trays of cookies between the top and bottom racks of a conventional oven midway through baking. If your microwave does not have a carousel or turntable, rotate the platter one to three times during the cooking for more even results.

Liquids do not evaporate as rapidly in a microwave oven as they do in a conventional oven. For that reason, dough and papier-mâché items need to be turned periodically, and flower petals need to be stirred (but not whole blossoms in silica gel, which absorbs moisture). Moisture often collects at the base of an object made of clay or papier-mâché, so setting it on top of two paper towels helps. Steam can also build up in a wet papier-mâché creation, so do not cook it for longer than the recommended times – the pressure could cause it to explode.

TESTING CONTAINERS IN THE MICROWAVE

To test whether a container is microwave safe, put 1 cup (8 ounces) of water in a glass measuring cup. Place the cup in or immediately next to the container in the oven, then cook on High for 1 minute. If the container is cool, it is safe. If it is hot, do not use it.

If you cook food in a microwave, you already know the rules about containers, but they bear repeating. Never use metal. Microwaves cannot penetrate metal, and the substance inside will not cook. More dangerous, metal can cause the microwaves to arc and start a fire that could possibly ruin your oven. This rule goes beyond the obvious metal pot: Don't use the fancy iron pots coated with enamel; don't use a nonmetallic container with metal handles or trim, metallic glaze, or silver or gold paint.

Here is what you can use: Heat-tempered glass, clay, or ceramics; microwave-safe plastic or rubber; or cardboard (I use shoeboxes in which to dry flowers). Although microwaves do not heat the container, the substance in it will transmit heat to the container. If the pot or bowl is made of glass that is not heat-tempered or plastic that is not microwave safe, the heat of the substance being cooked may crack or possibly melt the container.

Some cooks occasionally use small pieces of foil to shield parts of an item that might otherwise cook too fast – the wingtip on a piece of chicken, for example, or a tiny dough leaf protruding from a piece of dough fruit. Do this, however, only with extreme caution. Check the owner's manual, as even the smallest piece of foil cannot be used in some models. If the handbook says small pieces of foil are OK, make sure the foil is flat and smooth. It cannot be crumpled, folded, or otherwise touch itself, or it may cause arcing and a fire. The foil cannot touch the walls of the oven either. And, after all those precautions, you may find the blower will dislodge it anyway.

Do not be intimidated by all these warnings. Just use caution, as you would with any unfamiliar tool or appliance. Make frequent tests and experiments, and become comfortable with your microwave oven. As your skills with microwave crafts grow, your creativity will blossom.

CHAPTER ONE

drying flowers, leaves, and herbs

ABOVE *Microwave-dried flowers in waiting – even before they are arranged, they make a delightful composition with their clear, bright colors and variety of textures. Those in the basket include peonies, sea-lavender, quaking grass, love-in-a-mist, larkspur, rosebuds, straw-flowers, statice and lady's-mantle.*

Think of the joy of the first daffodil of spring, or the glory of brilliantly colored autumn leaves. What pleasure they bring! Then, within weeks they are gone, withered and brown, and tossed onto the compost pile. By drying flowers and foliage in the microwave oven, you can preserve their beauty and extend enjoyment of them year round. And, as a bonus, in a single arrangement you can combine seasonal flowers and leaves that would otherwise never be seen together.

Dried flowers and foliage provide tremendous versatility – especially when collected throughout the year – combining spring tulips with autumn chrysanthemums, summer zinnias with Christmas poinsettias. They can be arranged in baskets and vases, attached to wreaths, glued to "trees" of cone-shaped foam, pressed and framed, and even used to decorate straw hats and brooms.

Your garden is probably full of flowers you can dry in the microwave. Some of the most popular – and easily grown – flowers are prime candidates for drying: Zinnias, daisies, roses, chrysanthemums, hydrangeas, baby's-breath, primroses, marigolds, calendulas, and strawflowers are among them. Boughs of silver-dollar eucalyptus are eye-catching additions; autumn leaves add wonderful colour to all sorts of arrangements; and herbs also add visual interest – the pale green of sage, the purplish-red seedheads of oregano, tiny purple flowers on rosemary sprigs, the immature seedheads and feathery fronds of anise are but a few examples.

But roadside and wildland weeds usually not noticed – wild wheat and oats, sorrel, pampas grass, thistle, and papyrus – also become stars in dried arrangements.

Not all plants, however, are suited for microwave drying. The long stems of sorrel are too big for many ovens, for example. Bright red berries often burst in microwaves, and should, instead, be hung to dry for at least a week in a cool, dry, well-ventilated place. Fleshy flowers, such as magnolias and hyacinth, generally dry poorly and are not good candidates for dried arrangements.

COLOR AND THE MICROWAVE

Some flowers hold their color better than others when dried in a microwave. The brightest colors are most likely to stay true after drying. Others fade or develop a brown undertone. My marigolds and calendulas kept their bright yellows and oranges, while my gold chrysanthemums turned bronze, and the purple chrysanthemums took on a brown tinge. My deep-pink and white primroses turned a lovely shade of lavender, while the white stayed pure. Most white flowers turned to cream or got brown around the edges. White delphinium turned light blue, but white daisies, candytuft, and dogwood stayed white.

ABOVE *This beautiful microwaved cream rose shows the positive effect the drying process can have on the colors of the plant materials.*

LEFT *Displayed here are the basic ingredients needed for microwave drying. The white granules in the glass bowl are silica gel, the substance thought to be the most effective drying agent, which can also be used over and over.*

CREATING COLOR

You do not have to limit yourself to the colors nature provides. Some flowers, including baby's-breath, straw-flowers, hydrangeas, yarrows, and goldenrods, can be colored easily with fabric dye. The most common method is to dissolve powdered dye in boiling water and immerse the dried flowers for 10 minutes or longer, or you can follow the directions on the dye package. Some items, including holly leaves, eucalyptus, nuts, and pine cones, take on a new beauty when colored with spray paint – particularly silver, gold, and white.

Microwave drying is not a difficult or expensive process, especially if you cut flowers from your garden and scavenge roadside weeds and grasses. But, start slowly and experiment with different techniques and microwave settings until you develop a good sense of what works in your microwave. Also, remember dried leaves and flowers are brittle, and your fingers are apt to be clumsy until you get the hang of wiring them – you will discard quite a few broken flowers and leaves in the beginning.

When harvesting leaves and flowers for drying, here are a few tips worth remembering:

- Flowers should be not quite at their peak of bloom.
- Flowers in full bloom often lose their petals during drying.
- Do not pick flowers for drying while they are still dewy or wet from rain, they should be dry.
- Or, let flowers stand in a vase, if necessary, until dry.
- Zinnias, chrysanthemums, and daisies are excellent flowers for beginners, as are flat leaves like maple and elm.

Trim off all but an inch or so of the stem before drying. (Most dried flower stems are extremely fragile and crumble away when you handle them.) After the flowers are dry, you will create a replacement stem with wire and tape. If the flower has a thick stem – like the zinnia, for example – insert a toothpick point all the way through the top of the stem, perpendicular to the stem. After the flower is dried, the toothpick must be removed so that wire can be threaded through the hole to make a reinforced stem (see pages 22 to 24).

The best method of drying foliage uses silica gel, which is actually not a gel, but granules that look and feel like sugar. Silica gel can absorb 40 percent of its weight in moisture, so it works faster than cornmeal and borax, and is less likely to cling to petals and leaves after drying.

Silica gel can be used over and over for

THE OPEN METHOD OF DRYING HERBS, LEAVES, AND FLOWERS

Herbs, leaves, and flowers can also be dried in the microwave without any drying agent. This method is preferable in certain circumstances, such as when you're drying flowers for potpourri, or herbs for a wreath, and may want to use the herbs in cooking later. It is also better to dry unopened rosebuds this way, since the silica will not penetrate to the bud's center, and aggravates uneven drying. When the open method is used, it is better to dry the herbs in batches, one type at a time, since most require different drying times. Cooking times vary from 4 to 6 minutes for fragile leaves like basil, to 10 minutes for sage and rosemary.

The disadvantage of the open method is that it takes two to four times as long as the silica gel method. Also, the flowers tend to lose their shape or become badly shrivelled, making this method best for herbs and some leaves.

ABOVE *Some herbs, leaves, and flowers can be dried without any drying agent but they need to be dried in small batches and one type at a time. The disadvantage is that this method takes longer than if silica gel is used.*

years. When the crystals in the mixture are saturated with moisture, they turn pink. Then, spread a layer of silica gel on a tray or shallow baking pan, place in a conventional oven at 250°F and cook for about 30 minutes, until the pink crystals turn blue again. Cool, then store in an airtight container.

Silica dust, inevitable when you are pouring silica gel, can irritate your nose and throat, so work in a well-ventilated room. You may want to use an inexpensive filter mask over your nose and mouth, the type you would use to avoid breathing in dust created by sanding plasters, available at hardware stores.

You may also use cornmeal or borax or a mixture of the two, but they take roughly 50 percent longer to dry than silica gel, and tend to stick to flowers, especially ones with fine hair or fuzz. Cornmeal and borax can be reused, although they do not last as long as silica gel. Cooking times vary widely, depending on the type of microwave, the type and quantity of flowers, and the heat retained by silica gel in continuous use. Experiment until you get consistent results. I use a Medium-Low setting of 40 percent power, but that setting will not work in all microwaves.

Then, just as food cooked in a microwave oven continues cooking for a few minutes after it comes out of the oven, the flower-drying process continues after they are removed from the oven. Let flowers and leaves sit undisturbed in the silica gel for at least 10 minutes. Large, heavy flowers or leaves benefit from sitting for longer periods.

DRYING FLOWERS IN THE MICROWAVE

YOU WILL NEED

Silica gel
Microwave-safe dish
Florist's scissors
Small spoon
Small, soft paintbrush
Wire cooling rack

Selection of fresh flowers

1 Pour a 1-inch layer of silica gel into a microwave-safe dish.

2 Trim off all but about 1 inch of the stem from the flowers to be dried.

3 Insert the stems into the silica, then the flowerheads. If the silica is not sufficiently deep to support the flowers, spoon additional silica around their bases.

4 Gently spoon additional silica gel over flowers tops until they are completely covered.

5 Place the dish into the microwave. Cooking times vary widely, depending on the type of microwave, the type and quantity of flowers, and the heat retained by silica gel in continuous use. Experiment until you get consistent results; see pages 20 to 21 for guidelines. Once the dish is out of the microwave, leave the flowers undisturbed for at least 10 minutes.

6 Carefully pour some of the silica gel off the flowers, until they can be removed quite easily.

7 Using a small, soft paintbrush, gently brush off silica granules; stubborn granules will probably fall off on their own later. Petals and leaves are very brittle at this point, and are easily broken by the brushing motion. Set the flowers on a wire cooling rack to protect the shapes.

POSITIONING FLOWERS IN SILICA GEL

There are two ways to position flowers in silica gel. All open-faced flowers such as pansies, carnations, roses and daffodils should be placed upright in the silica to ensure that the flower is covered inside and outside with silica. Imagine it as a cup that needs to be filled. All sprays such as statice, lily-of-the-valley, and jasmine should be laid horizontally in the silica gel.

DRYING HERBS IN THE MICROWAVE

YOU WILL NEED

Silica gel
Microwave-safe dish
Small spoon
Wire cooling rack
Selection of fresh herbs

1 Pour a 1-inch layer of silica gel into a microwave-safe dish. Place a herb sprig, such as rosemary, on the granules.

2 Gently spoon additional silica over the herb until it is completely covered. You can dry 2 kinds of herbs simultaneously by placing 2 dishes in the microwave at the same time.

3 Place the dish or dishes into the microwave. Cooking times vary widely, so experiment until you get consistent results. Once the dishes are out of the oven, leave the herbs undisturbed for at least 10 minutes.

4 Carefully pour some of the silica gel off the herbs until they can be easily removed. Using a small, soft paintbrush, gently brush off silica granules; stubborn granules will probably fall off on their own later. Set the herbs on a wire cooling rack until ready for use.

DRYING LEAVES IN THE MICROWAVE

YOU WILL NEED

Silica gel
Microwave-safe dish
Small spoon
Small, soft paintbrush
Wire cooling rack

Leaves

1 Pour a 1-inch layer of silica gel into a microwave-safe dish. Lay the leaves on the granules. Gently spoon additional silica gel over the leaves until they are completely covered.

2 Place the dish into the microwave. Cooking times vary, see page 21 for guidelines. Once the dish is out of the oven, let the leaves sit undisturbed for at least 10 minutes.

3 Carefully pour some of the silica gel off the leaves, until they can be easily removed.

4 Using a small, soft paintbrush, gently brush off silica granules; stubborn granules will probably fall off on their own later. Set the leaves on a wire cooling rack to protect their shape until ready to use.

DRYING FLOWERS

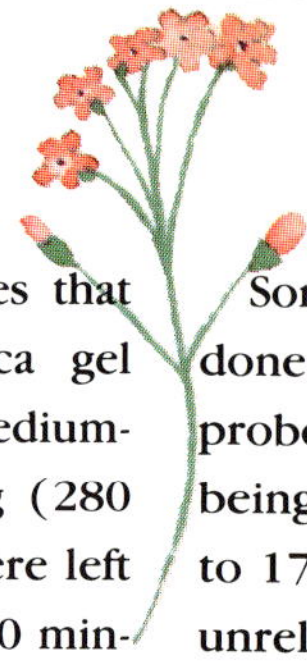

Here are a few examples of times that worked for me, using the silica gel method. All were heated at the Medium-Low power (40 percent) setting (280 watts in a 700-watt oven), and were left to stand undisturbed for at least 10 minutes after they came out of the microwave.

Some people recommend testing for doneness by inserting a temperature probe into the silica gel, with most items being dried when the gel measures 150°F to 175°F. I found this method extremely unreliable, especially when silica is warm from repeated use in a short time.

FLOWERS	QUANTITY	BOX SIZE	AMOUNT OF SILICA GEL	TIME
ARTEMISIA	4 stems	10- × 6- inches	3 inches	3 minutes
ASTER	5 asters, 2 inches diameter	10- × 6- inches	3 inches	4½ minutes
BABY'S-BREATH *(Gypsophila)*	2 stems	10- × 6- inches	3 inches	3 minutes
CAMPION *(Silene)*	4 stems	10- × 6- inches	3 inches	3½ minutes
CANDYTUFT *(Iberis)*	4 stems	10- × 6- inches	3 inches	3½ minutes
CARNATION *(Dianthus)*	3 carnations, 1½ inches diameter	4- × 4- inches	3 inches	3½ minutes
CHINESE LANTERN * *(Physalis alkekengi)*	6 lanterns, cut open	10- × 6- inches	3 inches	4½ minutes
CHRYSANTHEMUM	3 button mums 8 mums	4- × 4- inches 10- × 6- inches	3 inches 3 inches	5 minutes 7½ minutes
CORNFLOWER *(Centaurea cyanus)*	4 cornflowers	4- × 4- inches	3 inches	2½ minutes
COSMOS	3 cosmos	4- × 4- inches	3 inches	2 minutes
DAISY	5 Gloriosa daisies	10- × 6- inches	3 inches	3½ minutes
GLOBE AMARANTH *(Gomphrena globosa)*	4 stems	4- × 4- inches	4 inches	4 minutes
GOLDENROD *(Solidago)*	4 stems	10- × 6- inches	3 inches	3½ minutes
HYDRANGEA	1 cluster	4- × 4- inches	4 inches	4 minutes
LADY'S-MANTLE *(Alchemilla mollis)*	2 stems	10- × 6- inches	3 inches	3½ minutes
LARKSPUR	4 stems	10- × 6- inches	3 inches	3½ minutes
LAVENDER *(Lavandula)*	4 stems	10- × 6- inches	3 inches	3½ minutes
MARIGOLD *(Tagetes)*	5 marigolds 10 marigolds	4- × 4- inches 10- × 6- inches	3 inches 3 inches	3 minutes 6 minutes
NOTCH-LEAF SEA LAVENDER *(Limonium bellidifolium)*	4 stems	10- × 6- inches	3 inches	3 minutes
PANSY *(Viola tricolor)*	8 pansies	10- × 6- inches	2 inches	2½ minutes

*air dry by hanging if lanterns are to remain closed

FLOWERS	QUANTITY	BOX SIZE	AMOUNT OF SILICA GEL	TIME
PRIMROSE *(Primula)*	1 large cluster	4- × 4- inches	4 inches	4 minutes
RHODANTHE	4 stems	10- × 6- inches	3 inches	3½ minutes
ROSE *(Rosa)*	6 roses (thin petals and not fully open) 1 rosebud 3 miniature roses	10- × 6- inches 4- × 4- inches	4 inches not recommended 3 inches	5½ minutes use "open" method 3½ minutes
STATICE *(Limonium)*	5 stems	4- × 4- inches	4 inches	3 minutes
STRAW-FLOWER *(Helichrysum bracteatum)*	3 straw-flowers 8 straw-flowers	4- × 4- inches 10- × 6- inches	3 inches 3 inches	3½ minutes 6 minutes
YARROW *(Achillea)*	3 stems	4- × 4- inches	4 inches	3½ minutes
ZINNIA	3 zinnias 5 zinnias	10- × 6- inches 10- × 6- inches	3 inches 3 inches	4 minutes 5 minutes

LEAVES AND GRASSES

Because leaves are flat, you can stack 2 to 3 layers of leaves and silica gel in a box.

PLANT	QUANTITY	BOX SIZE	AMOUNT OF SILICA GEL	TIME
Lightweight leaves such as: **MAPLE** **ELM** **STRAWBERRY** **ROSE** **CHRYSANTHEMUM** **SAGE**	1 layer 3 layers	10- × 6- inches 10- × 6- inches	1 inch 3 inches	3 minutes 7 minutes
Thicker leaves such as: **CAMELLIA** **BAY LAUREL** **HOLLY**	1 layer 3 layers	10- × 6- inches 10- × 6- inches	1 inch 3 inches	5½ minutes 11 minutes
Coiled spray of **IVY**	12-15 leaves	10- × 6- inches	3 inches	10 minutes
SILVER-DOLLAR EUCALYPTUS	2 stems	10- × 6- inches	3 inches	10 minutes
Wild grasses such as: **OATS** **WHEAT** **BARLEY**	4-6 stems	10- × 6- inches	3 inches	5 minutes
BAMBOO	1 layer 3 layers	10- × 6- inches 10- × 6- inches	1 inch 4 inches	3 minutes 5½ minutes

MAKING STEMS

YOU WILL NEED

Toothpick
Wire cutters
Floral tape
Fine-gauge floral wire
Medium-gauge floral wire

WIRING CARNATIONS

1 Make a hole at the top of the stem with a toothpick, then remove the toothpick. Using medium-gauge floral wire, thread about 1 inch of wire through the hole.

2 Bend the wire over and down the length of the stem. Cut the other end of the wire to the length of the stem you wish to create – about 6 inches. Beginning at the flower's base, wrap the wire and the natural stem with floral tape held at an angle. Continue wrapping down the wire, stopping short of the bottom if it will not be visible in the completed arrangement. Cut tape.

WIRING A STRAW-FLOWER

1 Hold a 4- to 5-inch piece of medium-gauge floral wire at the flower's base. Carefully poke the wire up through the center of the flower. Bend the wire in the middle, and poke the end back through the center, creating a loop. If the flower has a fuzzy center, the wire should be invisible. It is a good idea to prepare several flowers in this way before commencing a design.

WIRING A DRIED ROSE

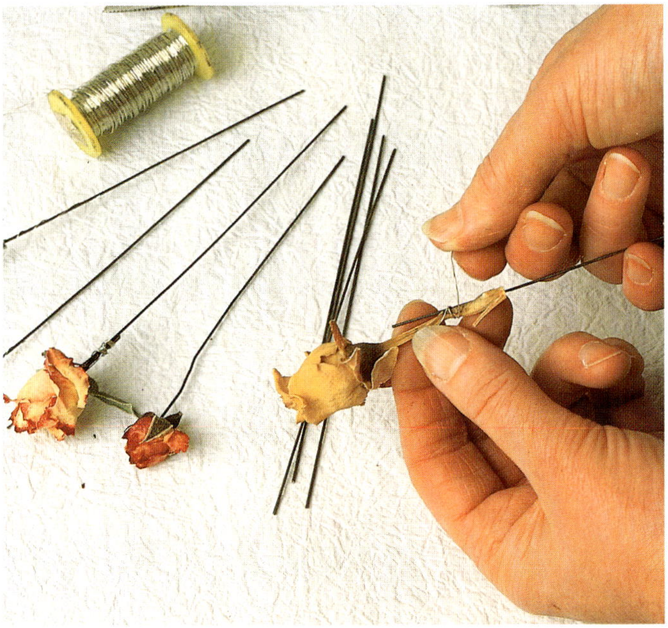

1 Bind a medium-gauge wire onto the short stem with fine-gauge floral wire.

2 Bind the entire false wire stem with floral tape to secure.

WIRING A DRIED ORCHID FLORET

Hold a 4- to 5-inch piece of fine-gauge floral wire at the base of the flower. Carefully bind on the false stem with fine-gauge floral wire.

WIRING HYDRANGEAS

This is simply done by inserting clusters of dried hydrangea florets onto a hollow straw stem.

WIRING CORNFLOWERS

Hold a 4- to 5-inch piece of medium-gauge floral wire at the base of the flower, then carefully bind on the false stem with fine-gauge floral wire.

WIRING HERBS

Because dried herbs are brittle and so often snap and break when you stick a pin through them, it is easier to pin leaves and herbs when they are only partially dry, then leave them to air dry. If you have fresh branches of rosemary, for example, bend them to the shape of the wreath and attach them, then leave to air dry.

CHAPTER TWO

wreaths

Once you have a good-sized cache of dried flowers, you are ready to make your first arrangement. Wreaths are a good first project because the flowers do not always need stems – they can be glued directly onto a store-bought wreath form. Also, flowers and leaves can be overlapped to hide mistakes and broken edges, and best of all, the arrangement's basic shape is already set.

Inexpensive various-sized forms can be bought at craft stores. If you want to leave a portion of the form uncovered, grapevine or willow wreaths are a good choice, straw or moss forms are also attractive enough to leave partly bare. Foam bases, however, should be completely covered. You can wind ribbon or raffia around a wreath form, or cover it with moss before attaching flowers.

You can also buy double-ring wire bases and stuff them with moss, straw, or pine needles; make your own grapevine forms by weaving fresh and supple vines into wreaths, then letting them dry. Or, when you feel confident, make a base from scratch: Make a single loop of heavy wire, arrange fistfuls of straw in a circle around the loop, then wind fine-gauge floral wire around the straw and wire loop to secure them together.

If you plan to attach heavy items to a section of the wreath, use wire to secure a block of foam to the wreath form. The foam gives greater support to disproportionately heavy items.

Before you start gluing items to the wreath, lay them out in a rough approximation of the final arrangement, then move items around until you are satisfied with the design. Generally, you should attach the largest and heaviest items to the wreath first, the smallest or lightest items last.

Begin by arranging sheets of newspaper over your work surface. If your glue gun does not have a stand, you will need a glass plate or a nonflammable, preferably nonmetallic, dish to set the hot gun on.

Most of the wreaths in this book can also be made with 8-inch or 10-inch forms, and can even be used to display candles (see Christmas Candle Wreath and Candleholder Wreath).

ABOVE *A selection of wreaths, rings, and bases you are able to buy or make. From top left, clockwise, twisted grass stem wreath, corn dolly wreath, absorbent foam ring, twisted-twig ring, and the same ring spray-painted.*

ABOVE *To make a hook for hanging a wreath, you use 1 medium-gauge floral wire. Bend it to make a U-shape and twist the 2 ends beneath it. Push the wire ends through the outer ring or the frame and bend them back to secure.*

FALL LEAVES WREATH

This is an excellent project for beginners because it uses readily available foliage – at least during fall when leaves are turning color. It is also one of the most basic and simple arrangements.

YOU WILL NEED

10-inch grapevine wreath
Glue sticks and a glue gun
Fine-gauge floral wire

Small pine cones
A selection of pressed flowers and some leaves, such as grape leaves, dried in silica gel
Poppy and other seedheads
Beech masts
Sycamore "wings"
Hops
Dried mushrooms
Selection of various-sized dried fall leaves

Glue the cones to the top center of the wreath; if the cones are large or heavy, attach them with wire. If you have a few smaller cones on stems, such as alder cones, attach so they dangle in the center of the wreath; you can also glue little cones scattered through the leaves.

Next, make sprays of small leaves and bind them with the floral wire, then glue them around the wreath. Be sure to balance the color selection around the wreath form.

Then, beginning at the center top, around the cones, attach individual leaves, largest leaves first, alternating colors and shapes in a haphazard way. Glue small leaves over large ones, overlapping each leaf over the next. Continue until the wreath form is covered.

Using the glue, attach remaining components, such as seedheads, hops, beech masts, mushrooms, and sycamore "wings." Make sure they are evenly distributed around the wreath.

PINK AND PURPLE WREATH

Built on a willow or grapevine form painted white, this wreath has a light and airy character that is set off by purple and pink dried flowers and ribbons woven around the form. The type of flowers you use here is not as important as the colors.

YOU WILL NEED

10-inch grapevine wreath
White paint
3 yards each pink and purple ribbons
Glue sticks and a glue gun
Fine-gauge floral wire
Medium-gauge floral wire
Selection of dried flowers, herbs, seedheads, and foliage, such as purple-dyed poppy seedheads, purple sage leaves, eucalyptus, marjoram flowers, sea-lavender, thistles, statice, mixed foliage

Paint the wreath and leave to dry; because of all the twists and hard-to-reach spots, it will probably require 2 coats.

Weave 1 of the ribbons around the wreath form, ending with a knot at the back of the wreath.

Lay out the seedheads, flowers, and foliage around the wreath form. The foliage should not completely cover the form – plenty of white grapevine and ribbon should show through.

Then, beginning with the leaves and larger flowers, glue and wire the foliage to the wreath. Then glue the seedheads in prominent positions. Finally, take the remaining ribbon and make it into a bow, then attach it to the wreath at the top, somewhat off center, by pushing a medium-gauge floral wire bent into a U-shape through the loop at the back of the bow and twisting the ends together. Press the wire into the wreath form.

RAFFIA WREATH

A large raffia bow on the side dominates this wreath. To balance the bow, thickly cover the wreath with flowers and foliage poking out in all directions. The wreath form is wrapped in raffia, with the color peeking out between the foliage.

YOU WILL NEED

2 yards apricot-colored raffia
10-inch double wire ring
Glue sticks and a glue gun
Fine-gauge floral wire
Medium-gauge floral wire
Selection of dried flowers and foliage, such as straw-flowers, baby's-breath, ming foliage, winged everlasting oats, carthamus, hydrangea leaves, lady's-mantle

Untwist the raffia, then wrap 1 yard of it around the wreath form, occasionally securing with glue; cover the form entirely. Fashion a large bow with the remaining raffia and attach it to the wreath form at the side with a medium-gauge floral wire.

Using fine-gauge floral wire, wire some flowers and leaves such as straw-flowers, baby's-breath, and lady's-mantle into small bunches. Lay the bunches around the wreath, and then glue them onto it. There should be enough large flowers and clusters to balance the raffia bow, and the stems of small flowers and leaves should protrude from the wreath to add depth and width. Glue the ming foliage and leaves to the wreath, beginning with the largest items. The foliage should be densely packed. If desired, add a small blossom or spray of flowers to the bow.

HERB AND SPICE WREATH

Dried bay leaves and garden herbs are used to create a good-smelling kitchen wall hanging in this wreath design. Because the star anise is glued to the wreath, it is not edible.

YOU WILL NEED

Medium-gauge floral wire
10-inch stem wreath form
Glue sticks and a glue gun
Raffia for bow

Green and red chilies and cinnamon sticks
Bay leaves
Star anise and garlic heads (air-dried)
Selection of other dried herbs, such as marjoram flowers, fennel stems and seedheads, curry plant, purple sage leaves

Take the fennel, marjoram, bay leaves, and seedheads, cut their stems short, and form them into mixed bunches. Bind the stems of each bunch with some medium-gauge floral wire and twist the ends tightly at the back.

Next, attach the bunches onto the wreath form at intervals by pushing the wire through the back of the wreath and bending it flat. Position the bunches so the design has a jagged and uneven outline.

Take the cinnamon sticks, garlic heads, and chilies and attach them singly or in small clusters to the wreath with medium-gauge floral wire.

Using the glue gun, glue the star anise to the wreath. Form a bunch of raffia into a bow and pin it onto the wreath.

HERB HINT

Use any herbs you wish for this wreath; the more variety, the better.

The chilies may burst in the microwave during drying, so cut a tiny slit in each back side, or prick in several places with a pin. Depending on their size, dry them for 10 to 20 minutes on Medium-Low power (40 percent).

For this project, the bay leaves need to dry flat instead of curly. Turn 1 pie plate upside down, cover with a paper towel, and arrange a single layer of bay leaves on top. Then cover with another paper towel and a second pie plate, right side up. (Note: You may dry another herb in the top plate at the same time.) Experiment with times; my microwave takes 20 minutes to dry a batch of bay leaves at Medium-Low power (40 percent).

WEDDING WREATH

Use this pretty white wreath, decorated with pale pinks and greens, as a lovely decoration for the door of the reception hall. I have suggested a pink and green color scheme, but the colors and types of flowers can be varied.

YOU WILL NEED

White paint
Pale green ribbon, ½-inch wide
10-inch grapevine wreath
White ribbon, ¼-inch wide
1 yard white tulle
Birdseed
Medium-gauge floral wire

Selection of dried flowers, such as baby's-breath, jonquils, daffodils, Peruvian lilies, hydrangeas, rosebuds

Paint the wreath form and leave to dry. It will probably require at least 2 coats.

Wrap pale green ribbon around the wreath form, ending with a bow at the bottom.

Cut the tulle into circles, using a saucer as a template, then put a small amount of birdseed in the center of each, and tie with white ribbon. Using a second piece of white ribbon, tie the pouches to the bottom of the wreath form.

Arrange flowers and leaves along the top and down the sides. Beginning with leaves and the largest flowers, take the medium-gauge floral wire and wire the foliage to the wreath.

CHRISTMAS WREATH

The spicy smells of December are as much a part of the holidays as the traditional colors of red and green. This wreath incorporates the best of both, with eucalyptus and cinnamon sticks providing a delightful melange of scents, and Chinese lanterns and ribbon providing orange accents.

YOU WILL NEED

Fine-gauge floral wire
10-inch grass stem wreath
Medium-gauge floral wire
Raffia
Orange ribbon
Cinnamon sticks
Dried Chinese lanterns
Selection of dried evergreen foliage, such as eucalyptus, yew, box, ivy

First make bunches of mixed eucalyptus, yew, box, and ivy, binding them with fine-gauge floral wire. Attach them to the wreath form with the medium-gauge floral wire so that they overlap in pairs, with the head of 1 bunch placed against the head of another. This way the stems are covered, and the design is built up and given depth and width. Continue until the wreath is completely covered with the evergreen materials.

Then, taking the cinnamon sticks, make bunches with medium-gauge floral wire and push these into the wreath base. Attach the Chinese lanterns in the same manner, between the evergreens.

Finally, make a bow with the ribbon; bend some medium-gauge floral wire into a U-shape and push it through the loop at the back of the bow and twist the ends together. Press the wire into the wreath form.

COUNTRY WREATH

The sweet smells of a flower potpourri are combined with the country look of gingham or calico in this traditional-style wreath.

YOU WILL NEED

½ yard printed cotton
Potpourri (see pages 63 to 76)
Twine
Fine-gauge floral wire
10-inch stem wreath
Medium-gauge floral wire
Rough-weave ribbon, 1-inch wide

Selection of dried flowers and foliage, such as carthamus, marjoram, baby's-breath, sea-lavender, oats, wheat, larkspur, cornflowers

First assemble the potpourri pouches. Using a saucer as a template, cut out 5 5-inch circles from the printed cotton. Take a small amount of potpourri and place it in the center of each circle, then tie into a bundle using the twine. You may wish to stitch the bundles shut before tying.

With the fine-guage floral wire, tie the wheat and oats into small, separate bunches. Attach the potpourri bundles to the wreath form with medium-gauge floral wire by pushing it right through the back of the wreath form and flattening the ends against the wreath to secure them. Attach the bunches of wheat and oats in a similar way. Fill in the gaps with baby's-breath, sea-lavender, larkspur, and cornflowers. Make 2 multi-loop bows with the rough-weave ribbon (1 being larger than the other). Attach them to the wreath by bending the medium-gauge floral wire into a U-shape and pushing it through the loop at the back of the bow, twisting the ends together and pressing the wire into the wreath form.

CORN DOLLY

A semicircle of roses, lavender, straw-flowers, and marigolds are wired into the corn dolly, leaving part of the ring exposed.

First make small posies consisting of the straw-flowers, baby's-breath, sea lavender, oats, and cornflowers, securing them with the fine-gauge floral wire. Arrange the posies in a semicircle slightly more than halfway around the corn dolly ring. The semicircle should taper off rather than end abruptly. Then fasten the posies to the ring with the medium-gauge floral wire.

Fill in the gaps by simply pushing the rosebuds and any remaining baby's-breath into the ring.

Take the bright blue ribbon and make it into a bow and then, with a medium-guage floral wire bent into a U-shape, push it through the back of the loop. Tie the ends together and push into the ring.

YOU WILL NEED

8-inch corn dolly ring
Fine-gauge floral wire
Medium-gauge floral wire
18 inches bright blue ribbon, 1-inch wide

Selection of dried flowers and grasses, such as straw-flowers, cornflowers, rosebuds, baby's-breath, sea-lavender, oats

VALENTINE WREATH

A wreath to celebrate St. Valentine's Day, as well as romance the whole year round. Use whatever red, pink, and white flowers are available.

Wrap the ribbon around the twig form, ending at the center top with a multi-loop bow and letting the ends dangle; it is not necessary to cover all the twigs because this design allows the ribbon and twig base to show through.

Arrange the flowers around the twig form. They can be attached in one of 2 ways – by gluing single flowers to the form, or by wrapping fine-gauge wire around the stems of small bunches of flowers, then using medium-gauge floral wire bent into U-shapes to attach the flowers to the form. Depending on the type of flowers you choose, you will probably use both methods. Attach the largest flowers first, filling in with the smaller ones. Be sure to let the ribbon show through.

YOU WILL NEED

Decorative ribbon, 1-inch wide
10-inch long heart-shaped twig form
Glue sticks and a glue gun (optional)
Fine-gauge floral wire
Medium-gauge floral wire

Selection of dried flowers, such as rosebuds, baby's-breath, sea-lavender, straw-flowers, larkspur

CANDLEHOLDER WREATH

This asymmetrical candleholder makes a lovely centerpiece. The types of flowers and colors of the candles can create a homey, casual arrangement, or one for a more formal occasion.

YOU WILL NEED

10-inch florist's foam ring
3 candle spikes
3 candles
Wide gold ribbon
Medium-gauge floral wire

Selection of dried flowers, grasses, and seedheads, such as sea-lavender, statice, rosebuds, mini-rosebuds, curry plant, straw-flowers, poppy seedheads, thistles, oats, wheat

Take a foam ring base and set it on a table. Insert the 3 plastic candle spikes and insert the candles into them. If wished you can make bundles of the different grasses or push them individually straight into the foam by using their natural stems as they are sufficiently strong to be inserted. Cover the foam completely, filling in the gaps with the rest of the materials – rosebuds, mini rosebuds, straw-flowers, baby's-breath and curry plant.

Make the bow using wide gold ribbon. Push a medium-gauge floral wire bent into a U-shape through the back of the loop, twist the ends together, and push into the foam ring.

CHAPTER THREE

flower arrangements

ABOVE Because dried flower arrangements do not require water they can be arranged in hanging bouquets, wicker baskets, or in non-watertight boxes or weathered wood.

Dried flower arrangements have a beauty of their own, similar to fresh flowers but with unique characteristics. They have muted colors, a sense of timelessness, and an ability to extend the time of the seasons.

They also have great versatility. By substituting a few flowers or leaves, a dried-flower arrangement can be changed to fit your mood, a specific occasion, or a selection of new flowers that are the gift of changing seasons.

Because dried flower arrangements do not require water, the choice of settings and containers is huge. They can be arranged in hanging bouquets, placed in wicker baskets, or arranged in non-watertight baskets, or arranged in non-watertight boxes of weathered wood. And because the arrangements are long-term, if not permanent, it is worthwhile to paint or otherwise decorate the container to complement the flowers.

When choosing a container, consider the flowers and foliage to be used. The container must complement the flowers, not compete with them, and can range from the simplest terracotta saucer to an elaborately shaped and painted piece of pottery. Baskets of all shapes and sizes are inexpensive and versatile. Pottery, even an old piece inconspicuously chipped or cracked, is excellent. Wire bread baskets, brass buckets, clear fishbowls, old teapots, copper kettles, antique goblets, flowerpots, rattan wastebaskets, wood boxes, and even ordinary coffee mugs are all suitable candidates.

There are numerous ways a container can be decorated to complement an arrangement. Spray paint a basket a solid color, for example, or stripe it in colors that bring out the colors in the arrangement; cut out abstract shapes of paper in an array of colors, then glue them to a cracked flowerpot, and paint over with a clear varnish; cover a basket or pot with fabric that coordinates with the curtains, wallpaper, or bedspread in the room where the arrangement will sit; weave colorful ribbons through a basket; make a wire garland of the same flowers in the arrangement and tie it around the container; glue dried leaves from the arrangement to the outside of the pot and cover them with a clear varnish.

The setting also must be considered. Do not, for example, put a casual rattan basket of straw-flowers and daisies in a formal living room.

ABOVE The basic tools of flower arranging include: florist's foam in various shapes, a block dry florist's foam or some wire mesh, florist's tape, medium-gauge floral wire, and fine-gauge floral wire, and florist's scissors.

THE TOOLS OF FLOWER ARRANGING

To anchor the flowers and foliage, you need a florist's oasis, a block of dry florist's foam, or some wire mesh. Other materials, depending on the type of arrangement and anchor you use, include: a floral pin-holder or spike, floral clay, double-sided florist's tape, single-sided florist's tape, glue, fine-gauge floral wire, dried moss, a sharp knife, and wire cutters. Top-heavy arrangements may need to be balanced with pebbles or plaster of Paris in the bottom of the container.

Oasis is denser than foam, but allows wire stems to penetrate more easily. If you want to mix fresh flowers into a dried flower arrangement, the oasis can be soaked in water to keep those flowers alive and fresh.

A block of dry foam may be easier to find, but it is firmer than the oasis and may resist wire stems. You may have to work a little harder to poke the stems into dry foam, but it is a fine base and is widely used.

To shape the oasis or foam, place the container on top of it and press down hard enough to make an impression. Use a sharp knife to pare the oasis or foam to the appropriate shape, keeping it as close to the size of the container as possible. The foam should rise above the container's rim so you can insert flowers and foliage at all angles. If necessary, tape two blocks together to achieve the height.

Both the oasis and foam need to be anchored to the base of the container. You can glue them directly to the container, attach them with double-sided tape, or use glue or clay to attach floral spikes or pinholders, then impale the oasis or foam. If you are using a basket, use tape across the top. Just take a piece of wire, make a loop at one end to serve as a needle's eye, then thread the tape through, and use the wire "needle" to thread the tape through the basket's top. Crisscross the block with the tape.

Loosely crumpled or balled wire mesh works well in lightweight arrangements.

Wire mesh is attached to the basket with fine-gauge wire threaded through the mesh and the rim of the basket

Unless you are certain the flowers and foliage of your arrangement will hide any oasis, foam, or wire mesh entirely, cover it with dry moss.

DESIGN

Begin by remembering that rules are made to be broken. Following are some guidelines for mixing colors, choosing shapes, and finding balance, but all can be ignored, resulting in a striking arrangement. Use these guidelines only as a starting point, then bend and break them as you gain confidence in your creativity and your artist's eye.

When choosing flowers and foliage, look for a variety of shapes and textures, and remember most arrangements need fillers such as baby's-breath and grasses. These fillers create the shape and provide the backdrop for the stars of floral arrangements. Do you want leaves, other than the few that may still be attached to stemmed flowers?

ABOVE *This basket of dried lavender shows how effective a monochromatic color scheme can be.*

ABOVE A color scheme such as this bright array of contrasting colors is definitely among the most beautiful.

COLOR

Decide on a color scheme: Should it be monochromatic; related shades such as rust, red, and orange; or a bright array of contrasting colors? Contrasting colors are the most difficult to carry off successfully, but are among the most beautiful.

Do not forget to look to the setting and colors in the room where the arrangement will be placed. If wallpaper or upholstery fabric is accented with blue and orange, a floral arrangement with that often-difficult color combination is more likely to work. Remember also that autumn leaves can bring brilliant colors to an arrangement.

Consider non-floral ingredients to accent your creation. Pine cones, bundles of cinnamon sticks, bows, artificial clusters of berries, and a wide variety of store-bought novelties can be wired together to add to arrangements.

It is important for the size and shape of the arrangement to fit the setting. A centerpiece for the dining room table, for example, must be pleasing from all sides; a pot of flowers on a hall table may be flat on the backside; a bouquet on a sideboard should be flat on the backside; and an arrangement on the floor must be tall.

PROPORTION

When you begin to assemble an arrangement, look for proportion and balance. As a rule of thumb – at least for beginners – the height of the floral part of the arrangement should be one and a half to two times the container's height, or one and a half to two times as wide as the container. That rule can be extended if the tallest or widest component of the arrangement is feathery or airy. You should also consider the space the arrangement will occupy.

An arrangement does not need to be symmetrical to be balanced, but it should not look lopsided. This applies not only to the silhouette, but also to the arrangement's interior. Smaller and lighter flowers, for example, should outline the arrangement, while larger and heavier flowers should be closer to the center and base.

What will be the center of attention? The flower, bold leaf, or cluster of flowers you choose should be at the axis of the arrangement – the point at which the lines of the arrangement appear to converge. If your eye cannot follow the lines to a single point, the arrangement lacks balance.

Generally speaking, begin by outlining the shape with the tallest, lightest materials, and finish with the largest flowers to form the center or dominant point of the design.

RIGHT *When assembling an arrangement, look for proportion and balance. As a rule of thumb, the height of the arrangement should be about 1½ to 2 times as wide as the container.*

HANGING BOUQUETS

YOU WILL NEED

Fine-gauge floral wire
Florist's tape
Raffia

A selection of microwave-dried and air-dried flowers and foliage, such as lavender, larkspur, sea-lavender, baby's-breath, globe thistles, oats, linseeds

Here, I suggest two variations – one with an airy, spiky look, the other with a rounder, more dense appearance.

All the flowers should be on wired stems (see directions pages 22 to 24). Air-dry a few of the flowers or foliage to preserve their natural stems; natural stems help to disguise the wire-and-tape stems.

Unless the bouquets are to be carried, they should be arranged so they are nearly flat on the back, making it easier to hang them or lay them on a table. Begin with the longer stems and stalks, then add bunches of shorter stemmed flowers and foliage, placing each successive shorter bunch so it hides the wire-and-tape stems of taller ones.

When all the flowers and foliage are in place, bind some fine-gauge floral wire around the bunch to secure it. Cover the wire with raffia tied into a knot.

ALTERNATIVE HANGING BOUQUET

For the second bouquet, made with the same technique, I suggest a selection of dried flowers, such as larkspurs, roses, straw-flowers, sea-lavender, and hydrangea tied with a ¼-inch wide tartan ribbon.

FAN-SHAPED ARRANGEMENT

In this arrangement, the color of flowers is more important than the type. The combination of purple and orange, with green leaves, is the dominant characteristic of a traditional fan-shaped arrangement.

YOU WILL NEED

Woven basket with handle
Newspapers
White spray paint
Dry florist's foam
Ribbon, 1-inch wide

Selection of dried flowers and foliage, such as carthamus, straw-flowers, statice, sea-lavender, hydrangea, purple-dyed poppy seedheads, Chinese lanterns

The container should be approximately 5 to 6 inches tall, with an equal or slightly larger width. A fishbowl shape is ideal, as is a square basket. The container must be color coordinated, but if it is patterned, the print should be small and simple so it does not overpower the flowers. Try a wicker basket, spray-painted white, with purple and orange ribbons woven through the rim or glued around the rim.

Place a basket on the newspapers and spray it white: it may require 2 coats. Leave to dry for a few hours.

Fit the basket with the foam.

Decide on the arrangement's height and width. Position 3 stems of lavender, to form the points of a triangle – 1 pointing straight up in the center top, the other 2 pointing to the sides, at 45° angles from the top.

Loosely fill in the outline created by the 3 points with spiky or feathery material. Do the same working from the top down the front. Add some shorter spiky material such as statice, around the edge of the container.

Place 1 or 2 large flowers low in the arrangement, at the center front, to establish the visual center. Loosely fill in the front with more of the spiky or feathery flowers, alternating from one side to the other, to create a balance. Add any rounder flowers – such as hydrangeas – with the Chinese lanterns near the bottom, and the straw-flowers gradually blending into the background as you move higher. Allow some flowers to drip over the container's edge.

Repeat the process in the back, for a fully rounded arrangement if it is to be a centerpiece, and a flatter silhouette if it is to be placed against a wall. Tie a bow on the basket's handle.

COUNTRY BASKET

This arrangement lends a country look to any kitchen, bedroom, family room, or casual dining room. Use a shallow, square basket approximately $1\frac{1}{2}$ to 2 times as wide as it is tall.

YOU WILL NEED

Wire mesh
Rectangular basket
Florist's tape

Selection of dried flowers and foliage, such as statice, sea-lavender, cornflowers, rosebuds, love-in-a-mist, straw-flowers, carthamus, grasses, oats, wheat

Fix the wire mesh in the basket, then establish the height and width of the arrangement as described on page 41.

Begin with the oats, wheat and grasses, inserting the various types into the mesh, alternating from one side to the other.

Add greenery along bottom edge and work upward, decreasing the concentration near the top. Place the largest flowers near the bottom center, then work upward, gradually blending in smaller flowers such as rosebuds and cornflowers. Repeat the process on the back side.

STUDIED CASUAL

This arrangement has a wide fan shape similar to the Country Basket, but the selection of flowers gives it a rounder, denser feel. The container should be wider than it is tall, with a look that is neither formal nor as casual as a straw basket.

YOU WILL NEED

Ginger jar or other container
Dry florist's foam

Selection of dried flowers and foliage, such as mimosa, goldenrod, carnations, spray carnations, roses, larkspur, geraniums, hydrangeas, sedum, love-in-a-mist, baby's-breath, seedheads, feverfew, mixed foliage sprays

Fix the foam in the ginger jar and establish the height and width of the arrangement as described on page 41, using mimosa and goldenrod.

Loosely fill in with the flowers and baby's-breath. Add greenery around the bottom and work upward, using denser greenery near the bottom, and the lighter or smaller-leaved greenery near the top. Insert the largest roses in positions of prominence at center front.

Fill in with remaining roses, strawflowers, love-in-a-mist, and spray carnations, graduating to smaller blossoms toward the top and the outside.

GYPSY BASKET

Use an oblong basket, preferably one without sides and curved up at the edges, like a slightly bowed plate, and with a handle. The foliage spills over at both ends, emphasizing the long lines.

YOU WILL NEED

Flat basket, see above
Dry florist's foam
Fine-gauge floral wire
Plastic prong
Paper ribbon for bow

Selection of dried flowers and grasses, such as rosebuds, carthamus, straw-flowers, sea-lavender, hydrangeas, statice, larkspur, grasses

Slice off a rectangle of foam, about 1½ inches high, and attach it to the basket by encircling it at several points with fine-gauge floral wire. Thread the wire through the bottom of the basket, then twist the ends.

Insert some grasses at each end of the foam, so they spill over the basket's lips. Add the carthamus.

Follow with a mix of larkspur and more grasses, some of which are stuck in the top of the base, but are as near horizontal as possible. Each layer should be a little shorter so that it covers any wire stems of the layer below. Insert some pieces into the base sides, gently bending the wire stems so most point toward the ends, and a few short-stemmed pieces pointing sideways.

Finish covering the top of the base with grass, statice, and other flowers such as straw-flowers, sea-lavender, rosebuds, and hydrangeas on progressively shorter stems. The last few stems should be nearly upright.

Decorate the handle with a large colored paper ribbon bow.

SOMETHING WILD

Use grapevine leaves, grasses, and mimosa to emphasize the vertical lines of this arrangement. Choose a container taller than it is wide, such as a tightly woven wicker vase, a plain ceramic jar, or a pottery vase with a rough finish.

YOU WILL NEED

Earthenware jug, see above
Wire mesh
Fine-gauge floral wire
Florist's tape
Raffia to tie wheat stalks

Selection of dried flowers and foliage, such as peonies, straw-flowers, sea-lavender, baby's-breath, mimosa, roses, yarrow, grapevine leaves, grasses

Reinforce any stems that need reinforcement with the tape and wire (see pages 22 to 24).

Use crumpled wire mesh to anchor the stems in the earthenware jug.

Insert the tallest pieces of grass in the center, and loosely surround it with a few other pieces. Loosely fill in with more grasses, the shortest pieces at the outside. Bend a few stems of grass around the outside. Push the flowers in between the grasses aiming to place them in the center of the design with the heaviest concentration toward the bottom. This way the peonies, roses, and other flowers are well framed by the grasses which highlight the warm colors of the flowers.

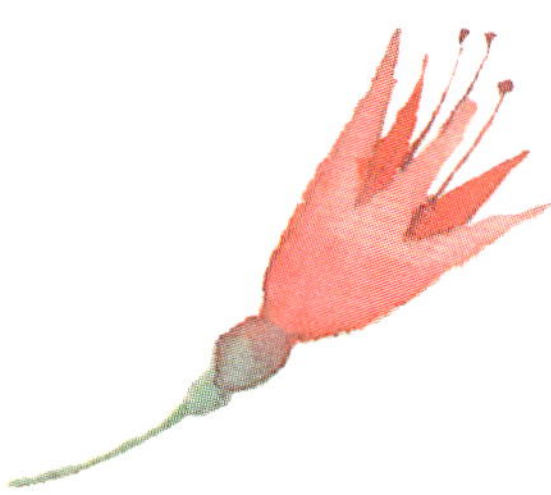

L-SHAPED ARRANGEMENT

This L-shaped arrangement uses few pieces, but they are large. A small table against a wall is a good setting. Use a small, shallow container, preferably one that is oblong. The height is defined by a single tall, dry apple twig.

YOU WILL NEED

1 pack florist's clay
Copper tray, see above
Glue (optional)
Plastic prong
Apple twigs
Pressed and wired hydrangea leaves

Selection of dried flowers and foliage, such as ming foliage, roses, daffodils, statice

Firmly attach the florist's clay base inside a shallow container; it needs to be tall enough to support the apple twigs but there will be scant foliage to hide it, so strike a careful balance.

Insert 1 apple twig into the base, then another branch in front, and to the side of it. The branch in front should be shorter than the one in the back, but its twisted shape adds width. A little glue in the base holes may help secure them.

Add a few upright stems of ming foliage, then a few horizontal ones of varying lengths to create the L-shape.

Add some upright and horizontal sprays of roses and daffodils, which should be slightly shorter than the statice.

Finish by attaching 3 to 4 large hydrangea leaves, 1 at the axis of the arrangement, and 1 each on the horizontal and vertical lines.

WALL BASKET

Arranged in a flat-backed basket or sconce, this creation is designed to hang on the wall. A single large arrangement looks nice, as do a pair of smaller, matching ones. If you use a natural color basket, consider spray painting it a glossy white or pastel that coordinates with your decor and the color of the flowers.

YOU WILL NEED

Wall basket
White spray paint
Wire mesh
Fine-gauge floral wire
Florist's tape
Ribbon, ½-inch wide

Selection of dried flowers and foliage, such as cornflowers, sea-lavender, statice, larkspur, straw-flowers, baby's-breath, globe thistles

Spray the basket white and leave to dry: it will probably require 2 coats.

To keep the arrangement light, use a crumpled wire mesh base wired to the basket.

Insert several sprays of larkspur and statice that hang over the basket's front and sides, and a few upright sprays. Add the baby's-breath and sea-lavender, so that it is more or less evenly distributed through the design.

Then dot the cornflowers, straw-flowers, and globe thistles around the arrangement so the colors are balanced.

CHAPTER FOUR

other dried flower projects

CHRISTMAS GARLAND

Like the Christmas Wreath, this garland combines the colors and scents of the holidays using potpourri and gold holly. Drape the garland over a doorway, a window, or a hearth.

YOU WILL NEED

Scissors
Red velvet
Walk in the Woods potpourri (page 70) or other potpourri
Color-coordinated ribbon, ¼ inch wide
Green binding twine
Gold spray paint
Fine-gauge floral wire
Rope or thick cord
Ribbon, 2½ inches wide
Clay beads

Dry moss or hay
Holly leaves
Dried sprays of silver-dollar eucalyptus
Norwegian spruce
Dried ivy

To make potpourri pouches, cut the fabric into 8-inch circles. Put a small amount of potpourri in the center of each, then gather the fabric into a pouch. Sew the pouches closed, then tie with a narrow color-coordinated ribbon, leaving enough of a tail on each to tie it to wreath. I have used red velvet but you can use any Christmas fabric.

Cover the rope or thick cord with the dry moss or hay. Take a handful of hay, wrap it around the rope and bind it tightly over and over with the twine for the length of core you require.

Take the microwave-dried holly leaves and spray with gold paint. Leave them to dry. Wire into small bunches of about 4 leaves each.

Using fine-gauge floral wire, alternately attach eucalyptus, holly leaves, Norwegian spruce, ivy, and potpourri pouches to the rope. Overlap each attachment so it covers the wire of the previous item.

Wind the clay beads through the garland, securing at the ends with green binding tape. Place bows made from wide ribbon at intervals along the garland.

SPRING GARLAND

Much like the Christmas Garland (page 52), this spring decoration can be draped over doors or windows. Or it can be made in shorter pieces, tacked to a wall, and left to hang down in a straight line. Although I suggest a color scheme, pick whatever colors you want to coordinate with your decor – or your taste of the moment.

YOU WILL NEED

Thick raffia braid, 24 inches long
Fine-gauge floral wire
Medium-gauge floral wire
Ribbon, ½ inch wide
Raffia

Selection of dried flowers, such as baby's-breath, sea lavender, love-in-a-mist, hydrangea, lady's-mantle, cornflowers, statice

Attach 3- to 4-inch stems of medium-gauge floral wire to dried flowers. Wire flowers (except baby's-breath) into small bunches and tie ribbon bows onto every third or fourth bunch.

Using fine-gauge floral wire, attach the baby's-breath to the raffia braid. Attach flower bunches by sticking wire stems through the braid and bending back the ends to secure.

Tie on bunches of raffia at odd intervals along the length of the braid. Make a bow out of the remaining ribbon and attach it at the top of the garland.

FLORAL POMANDER & POTPOURRI POMANDER

Tie a sprig of mistletoe to the base of either of these pomanders, and you'll have a kissing ball!

YOU WILL NEED

Scissors
2 yards ribbon for each pomander
Florist's foam ball, 3 inches in diameter, for each pomander
Glue sticks and a glue gun
Medium-gauge floral wire
Dried lavender or potpourri
(pages 63 to 76)

Selection of dried flowers, such as straw-flowers, rosebuds
Fresh mistletoe (optional)

Cut the ribbon into 2 pieces of 30 inches and 42 inches. Tie each piece once around the foam ball, so the ribbons cross at right angles at the top and the bottom. Tie a bow at the top.

Dot the ball, one quarter at a time, with glue, then roll in dried lavender. Take care that the heat of the glue gun does not melt the foam ball. The ball does not have to be completely covered with lavender.

With medium-gauge wire, attach dried straw-flowers to the ball, until it is completely covered, including the portion of ribbon wrapped around the ball.

For an attractive and sweet-smelling pomander, use a similar technique to the floral pomander, but roll the glue-coated foam ball in crushed potpourri instead of lavender, then decorate it with rosebuds and mistletoe instead of strawflowers.

ORANGE POMANDER

Pomanders fill the air with a spicy fragrance. Here is one that is a little more elaborate than the traditional clove-studded orange.

YOU WILL NEED

1 orange
Florist's tape, ½-inch wide
Toothpick
Whole cloves
1 teaspoon ground cinnamon
½ teaspoon grated nutmeg
Small plastic bag
Tissue or waxed paper
1½ yards ribbon, same width as tape
Glue

Dried flowers, such as straw-flowers

Encircle the orange with 2 pieces of tape that cross at right angles at the orange's top and bottom. With a toothpick, pierce the orange skin, making rows of holes, each hole next to each other, up to the edge of the tape. Insert a clove in each hole. Remove the tape.

Put the cinnamon and nutmeg in a plastic bag and shake well. Put the orange in the bag and shake; tap to remove the excess spice. Loosely wrap the orange in tissue or waxed paper, and put in a dry, dark spot for 2 to 3 weeks.

When the pomander has dried, remove the tape and tie the ribbon where the tape was, with excess ribbon at the top. Glue small dried flowers on the ribbon around the orange. Tie sprigs of flowers in the ribbon at the top and bottom of the orange. If you like, you can tie a loop in the top end of the ribbon to hang the pomander.

HERB AND FLOWER TREE

This tree adds a pleasant herbal scent to a room while serving as a pretty centerpiece. Use as many different fresh herbs as you can find.

YOU WILL NEED

1 pack modeling clay or florist's hard-setting clay
Basket, 7 inches in diameter
Relatively straight tree twig, about 12 inches long
Foam ball, about 6 inches in diameter
Dry floral moss
Thin knife
Fine-gauge floral wire
1 yard calico, optional
Glue
Bright blue cord or ribbon, optional

Selection of fresh herbs, such as purple sage, sage, curry plant, marjoram, lavender
Selection of dried flowers, such as strawflowers, rosebuds, cornflowers, lady's-mantle, statice, hydrangea, love-in-a-mist, goldenrod, larkspur

Place modeling clay inside the basket. Insert the twig into the clay to form a "trunk."

Using a thin knife, cut a hole in the foam ball, barely wide enough for the "trunk" to fit in. Put a little glue on the top of the "trunk," then fit the foam ball onto the "trunk."

Dry the herbs one variety at a time, as they will have different cooking times.

Gather sprigs of herbs into small bunches and wind fine-gauge floral wire around the stems. Stick the wire-reinforced stems into the ball. Glue other leaves onto the ball, until it is covered and no plain surface is visible.

Use floral moss to cover the clay in the basket. If you wish, cover the exterior of the basket with calico, using glue to hold it in place. Decorate with bright blue cord or ribbon if you wish.

CONICAL TREE

This conical tree makes a nice springtime centerpiece – even if it isn't spring. Supplement the daisies with dried chrysanthemums and straw-flowers, if you like.

YOU WILL NEED

1 pack modeling clay or florist's hard-setting clay
Clay pot, 5 inches in diameter
Foam cone, 12 - 15 inches long
Relatively straight twig, about 12-inches long
Dry floral moss
Glue sticks and a glue gun
Thin knife
String, optional
Ribbon

Selection of dried flowers, such as straw-flowers, lady's-mantle, baby's-breath, goldenrod, achillea

Place the modeling clay in the clay pot. Insert the twig into the clay to form a "trunk."

Crush some of the moss into little bits. Apply glue sparingly to the cone, then roll the cone in the crushed moss until no plain surface shows. Using a thin knife, cut a hole in the base of the foam cone, barely wide enough for "trunk" to fit in. Put a little glue on top of the "trunk," then fit the foam cone onto the "trunk."

Apply the flowers in a random pattern, sticking their stems into the cone or using hot glue and a glue gun to attach them.

Alternatively, wind a piece of string around the cone, creating diagonal lines from top to bottom. Then use those lines as a guide for placing alternating rows of yellow and white daisies or similar flowers. Fill in spaces between flowers with straw-flowers and baby's-breath.

Use floral moss to cover the clay. Tie a ribbon in a bow around the twig at the base of the cone. You can also decorate the exterior of the pot, if you like, with extra flowers glued to the top and bottom.

MIRROR OR PICTURE FRAME

A photograph in a frame personalized with dried flowers is an ideal gift. Use this same technique to decorate a framed mirror.

YOU WILL NEED

Florist's foam
Mirror or picture frame
Heavy-duty, double-sided florist's tape
Fine-gauge floral wire
Medium-gauge floral wire
2 yards narrow satin ribbon

Selection of dried grasses
Selection of dried flowers, such as lady's-mantle, rosebuds

Cut a slice of florist's foam to fit the frame's upper corner. Attach it with double-sided tape. Then cut a second, smaller piece to fit the bottom corner at the opposite side, and attach it with double-sided tape.

Gather the grasses and flowers into tiny bunches, and wrap the stems with fine-gauge wire. Insert them into the upper foam block using medium-gauge floral wire bent into U-shapes, with the longest bunches pointing down toward the picture's center. Repeat on the bottom corner, with the longest bunches pointing up toward the center.

FLOWERED HAT

This hat is wearable, but the dried flowers are fragile, so use with care. A better alternative is to hang it on a wall. Choose colors that match your decor.

YOU WILL NEED

Straw hat
1½ yards velvet ribbon, 1-inch wide
Glue
Fine-gauge floral wire
Florist's scissors

Selection of dried flowers, such as sea-lavender, baby's-breath, hydrangea, rosebuds, larkspur, cornflowers, statice, mimosa
Dried artemisia foliage

Wind the ribbon around the crown of the hat, and tie a multi-loop bow at the rear. Attach with spots of glue.

Make tiny bunches of mixed flowers and foliage binding them with the fine-gauge floral wire.

To make a garland of the dried flowers, hold one of the tiny bunches against the floral wire, about 8 inches from the end of the wire. Wrap the wire around the stems, leaving a tail of about 6 inches of wire loose. Still grasping the wire, hold another bunch of flowers against it and wrap the stems, so the tips of the second bunch overlap the wire-wrapped stems.

Continue, alternating the flowers and overlapping each bunch, until the garland is long enough to reach around the hat crown. Leaving a 6-inch tail of wire at the end, cut the wire.

Wind the garland around the crown of the hat, twist the 2 wire tails together, and bend them under the garland. Hide the joint under the ribbon bow.

HORIZONTAL SPRAY

Hang this arrangement over a fireplace, a painting, a doorway, or a wall mirror, and add a sophisticated touch to any country-style decor.

YOU WILL NEED

Block florist's foam cut into 1 slice, 1-inch thick
Glue
Florist's moss
Medium-gauge floral wire

Selection of dried flowers, such as hydrangea, cornflowers, rosebuds, straw-flowers, sea lavender, sedum

Cover all but the backside of the foam with glue, then roll in the moss to camouflage it.

Wire a few of the longest stems of sea-lavender into 2 bunches, using the medium-gauge floral wire. Insert shorter stems into sides of foam block. Insert short stems of hydrangeas, cornflowers, straw-flowers, sedum, and sea lavender into the center.

Glue, or push, rosebuds and other long-stemmed flowers into the moss on the front, bottom, and top of the foam. Fill in with any remaining moss.

CHRISTMAS FLOWER BASKETS

Tiny baskets brimming over with dried flowers can be hung with a ribbon loop from the branches on your Christmas tree. If you wish, first put a little Walk in the Woods potpourri (page 70) in the bottom of the baskets for extra seasonal fragrance.

YOU WILL NEED

2 small woven baskets
Glue sticks and a glue gun
Small pieces ribbon, ¼-in wide
Potpourri, optional

Selection of dried flowers, such as baby's-breath, statice, sea-lavender, cornflowers

Fill the baskets with baby's-breath, securing with dots of glue if needed. Add statice, sea-lavender, and cornflowers.

Tie complementary colored ribbons around the baskets.

Finally, place a small amount of potpourri in the basket if wished.

CHAPTER FIVE

potpourri

ABOVE The secret behind potpourri lies in a mixture of dried flower petals, herbs, and spices whose perfumes are stabilized and refreshed by fixatives and oils.

Of our five senses, the most underrated is that of smell. Yet, smell is strongly evocative of our past. Who doesn't have memories tied to a high-school sweetheart's cologne or after-shave, a grandmother's lavender scent, the flowers that grew around a childhood home? The smells I grew to love in my childhood were the young blossoms on our backyard lemon tree, the deep red wild roses growing on our back fence, and the rose-scented potpourri on my grandmother's dresser.

Ancient civilizations were aware of the importance of fragrance. We know that the Greeks, Romans, and Egyptians used perfumed oils and incense several centuries B.C., and that by the sixteenth century, European households were strewn with sweet or spicy smelling leaves, while small bundles of leaves and flower petals were stored with linens.

Today's potpourri, a mixture of dried flower petals, herbs, and spices whose perfumes are stabilized and refreshed by fixatives and oils, actually dates to the eighteenth century. But today we have the advantage of time – with the microwave oven, we can dry flowers and leaves quickly, cutting the time needed to prepare potpourri.

In some respects, we are at a disadvantage. In return for better resistance to pests, disease, neglect, and poor growing conditions, many roses – the staple ingredient of most potpourris – have had their sweet smell bred out of them. This is especially true of hothouse roses. But a careful search will yield old-fashioned, strongly scented blossoms, and inexpensive oils are available to replace the natural perfume of modern roses.

While the main purpose of potpourri is its perfume, it can also be a pretty sight. For that reason, many modern potpourris include flowers, berries, and other items that have little if any scent, but that add color and beauty.

To make potpourris, look for a balance of scent and appearance. The gardenia, for example, has a lush scent, but its petals turn an ugly brown when dried. Azaleas, on the other hand, have slight odor, but the bright and pretty colors of their petals stay true through the drying process. With that in mind, many people decorate a finished dish of potpourri with whole dried blossoms, tiny pine cones, berries, and other eye-catching items. You can blend flowers on the basis of their colors.

LEFT A popular potpourri is one bearing a woodsy scent. The basic ingredients for this scent are conifer tips, small cones, allspice, whole cloves, and vanilla bean.

One of the delights of potpourri is the unseasonal combinations that can be created. Throughout the year, dry and store leaves and petals, then mix them at pleasure. Thus it is possible to have spring hyacinth mixed with winter evergreens, lilacs with late-summer marigolds.

The staple ingredient of traditional potpourris is the rose petal, plucked when the blossom is just past its peak bloom and rich with fragrance. Also popular are rose leaf and rose hip for contrast in color and texture, as well as whole dried rosebuds and small miniature blooms as decoration.

Other fragrant flowers are carnations, honeysuckle, jasmine, geraniums, marigolds, heather, sweet violet, lily-of-the-valley, hyacinth, crocus, woodruff, heliotropium, chamomile, larkspur, bachelor's button, and citrus blossoms, among others.

Not all potpourris are floral. Others are dominated by spicy, citrus, herbal, or woodsy scents. Cedar, mint, rosemary, pine, lemon, sandalwood, and patchouli are popular.

In addition to flowers and leaves, potpourris use sweet herbs, spices, fixatives, and oils.

Among the sweet herbs, lavender flowers are a staple of potpourris, but the leaf can also be used. Some health-food stores sell lavender.

Other herbs frequently used in potpourris are rosemary, mint, marjoram, lemon verbena, and thyme. Because these are commonly used in cooking, they can be purchased fresh from produce departments of well-stocked grocery stores, or sometimes in health-food stores. But most are also easy – and far less expensive – to grow yourself.

Most spices used in potpourris – cinnamon, nutmeg, cloves, allspice, mace, vanilla bean – are also readily available in grocery stores. Just keep in mind that spices lose their potency with age, so don't use nutmeg that has been sitting in your spice cabinet for three years.

Fixatives absorb the scented oils that perfume potpourri, and many add their own fragrance to the bouquet of scents. Without fixatives, the sweet fragrance of potpourri would quickly fade. At one time, animal fixatives like musk, civet, and ambergris were used. Today, orrisroot powder from a lily plant is the most common. If orrisroot powder is not available from your crafts store, try a drug store or a health-food store. Other fixatives – many potpourris use two – include gum benzoin, chamomile flowers, angelica seeds, cinnamon, nutmeg, myrtle, lemon verbena, and vanilla bean.

With the growing use of modern roses and pretty flowers that have little or no scent, the addition of oils is increasingly important, not only to refresh tired potpourris but to add fragrance to a just-made batch. Oils like lavender, rose, carnation, pine, sandalwood, and others are available at crafts stores.

Of the two methods used to make potpourri – dry and moist – the easiest and most common is the dry method, in which the petals are simply mixed with the other ingredients and allowed to ripen. But the moist method, which takes twice as many weeks and is much messier, produces strong fragrances that can last for years.

Potpourri still takes time – typically four to six weeks – to ripen, but you can cut down on the one to two weeks of drying time by using your microwave oven to dry flowers and leaves.

DRY METHOD OF MAKING MIXED FLOWER POTPOURRI

If you wish, you could decorate this with the pungent conical seed capsules of eucalyptus tree.

THE DRYING PROCESS

For the dry mix, begin with flowers that are not dewy or wet from rain; they will take longer to dry and dry unevenly.

The open method of drying flowers is used here, rather than the silica gel method as the silica tends to absorb fragrance.

Spread flowers or petals in a single layer in a microwave-safe dish. Cooking times will vary according to the type of microwave and the type and quantity of flower. Dry at Medium-Low power (40 percent) for 2- to 3- minute intervals, turning and stirring between intervals, until they are dry. Drying the petals can take 6 to 8 minutes for a small dish of geranium leaves, to 20 minutes for a large plate of rose petals. You may pluck the petals first, or dry the blossoms whole. I prefer the latter, so I can save the best-looking of the whole blossoms. As it becomes obvious that a whole flower won't look good dried, pull the petals out – they are easier and quicker to dry than whole blossoms.

YOU WILL NEED

¾ quart mixed dried flower petals
½ pint dried eucalyptus leaves
2 tbsp dried rosemary leaves
Peel of 1 lime, cut into small pieces and dried
20 whole cloves
1 tbsp orrisroot powder
2 drops lavender oil
2 drops rose oil
1 drop eucalyptus oil

When flowers, petals, or leaves are completely dry, mix your potpourri, or store them in an airtight container until you are ready to make potpourri. You can put a small amount of silica gel in the bottom of the container to absorb any remaining moisture.

To make the dry potpourri, begin by mixing the spices, fixatives, and oils. Rub the mixture together between your fingers to insure that the oils are absorbed. Then add the herbs and flower petals, and mix thoroughly.

Dry potpourri needs to be mixed and absorb scents for 4 to 6 weeks.

MOIST METHOD OF MAKING PURE ROSE POTPOURRI

Moist potpourri always begins with rose petals, but you can add smaller amounts of other fragrant flowers.

YOU WILL NEED

2 quarts rose petals, partially dried
2½ cups non-iodized salt

1 tbsp dried lavender
1 tbsp dried rosemary
1 tbsp orrisroot powder
1 tsp ground cinnamon
10 drops oil

THE DRYING PROCESS

Spread the petals on a microwave-safe platter and dry on Medium power (50 percent) for intervals of 2 to 3 minutes. Stop when the petals are half-dry and leathery. They need some moisture for the fermenting process.

Place 1 tightly packed cup of partially dried petals in a large, deep container and cover with ⅓ cup of non-iodized salt. Continue the layering, using ⅓ cup of salt for every 1 cup of petals. Some people add a pinch of sugar or a few drops of brandy to each layer to aid the fermenting process. Weigh down the mixture with a saucer or a stone, and cover tightly.

Leave the mixture to ferment for 6 weeks. If it bubbles, stir daily and drain water if any forms. Continue adding rose petals and salt during the first 4 weeks, but do not add any new materials for the last 2 weeks.

When the petals have formed a dry cake, break it into small chunks and add spices, fixatives, and oil(s). Store in an airtight container for another 2 to 3 weeks.

Moist potpourri isn't pretty so try to disguise it by setting it out in an opaque container, or crumble some in the bottom of a dish, then decorate it with dried flowers and petals, or cover it with dry potpourri.

EVERYTHING'S COMING UP ROSES

Decorate this traditional rose potpourri with dried rose leaves and whole dried rosebuds.

YOU WILL NEED

1 quart dried rose petals
Pinch fresh lavender
1 tbsp fresh rosemary spikes
¼ cup mixed geranium leaves and petals
1 tsp ground cinnamon
10 whole cloves
1 tbsp orrisroot powder
4 drops rose oil
1 drop lavender oil

Dry rose petals, lavender, rosemary, and geranium leaves and petals in the microwave, then mix together, following the directions for the Dry Method on page 66.

SPICY ROSE POTPOURRI

The spicy scents of carnation and marigold add variety to this rose-scented potpourri.

YOU WILL NEED

1 pint dried rose petal
1 pint mix of dried carnation, azalea, marigold
2 tbsp dried lemon verbena
1 tbsp dried thyme
1 tbsp orrisroot powder
3 drops rose oil
3 drops carnation oil

Mix all ingredients following the directions for the Dry Method on page 66.

SPRING GARDEN POTPOURRI

This potpourri is best displayed in brightly colored containers to lend atmosphere to its spring scent.

YOU WILL NEED

2 quarts partially dried rose petals
2 cups partially dried honeysuckle
2 cups partially dried lilac
4 cups non-iodized salt

1 tbsp dried lavender
1 tbsp dried lemon verbena
2 tbsp dried chamomile flowers
2 tsp ground cinnamon
1 tsp ground allspice
1 tsp orrisroot powder
12 drops rose oil, or a combination of rose and lilac oils

When the flowers are partially dried, layer and dry the potpourri following the directions for the Moist Method on page 67.

SWEET SPRING POTPOURRI

If you have some sweet-scented jonquils, add them to this mixture. You may substitute difficult-to-find lilac or jonquil oil for the rose oil.

YOU WILL NEED

1 pint dried hyacinth leaves
1 pint dried lilac
1 dozen large dried strawberry leaves
Pinch dried lavender
2 tbsp dried lemon verbena
1 tsp ground cinnamon
2 drops lemon oil
4 drops rose oil

Mix all ingredients together following the directions for the Dry Method on page 66.

WALK IN THE WOODS

Bright yellow and orange dried marigolds add color to this potpourri. If you want to use this in small pouches, consider crushing the cones and other large pieces.

YOU WILL NEED

¾ quart scented conifer tips, small cones, and small quantity of pine or fir needles
½ pint cedar shavings
½ pint dried marigolds
Peel of ½ lemon, cut into small pieces and dried
½ tsp ground allspice
20 whole cloves
½ vanilla bean, coarsely chopped
1 tbsp orrisroot powder
3 drops pine oil
2 drops cedar oil

Mix all the ingredients together following the directions for the Dry Method on page 66. As the needles tend to make this potpourri look messy, try and put them at the bottom of the dish when you display it.

THINGS TO DO WITH POTPOURRI

The most popular use for potpourri is to set it out in a pretty bowl, perhaps one painted with delicate and colorful flowers like those in the potpourri. Store it in a decorative corked jar, to be opened when the fragrance of the room needs to be refreshed. Place it in tightly woven baskets, open or lidded. Put some into a deep soap dish, then set small guest soaps in the potpourri – they will absorb the fragrance. Wrap clear or tinted cellophane around any of these arrangements, tie with a bow and decorate with a rose or sprig of spring flowers, and give as a gift. On the following pages are some other projects for you to try.

ABOVE All the equipment needed to assemble the potpourri projects featured on the following pages comes from a simple sewing kit: pins, needle and thread, a fabric of your choice, and some lace.

POTPOURRI AND POSY RING

This design takes the color, the texture, and the aroma of the flower mixture and transforms them into an irresistibly pretty decoration.

YOU WILL NEED

Glue sticks and a glue gun
6-inch straw wreath form
Potpourri
Medium-gauge floral wire
Fine-gauge floral wire
1 yard velvet ribbon, 1-inch wide

Selection of dried flowers, such as sea-lavender, baby's-breath, rosebuds, straw-flowers

Gather the dried flowers into a posy and cut the stems short, and bind them with a piece of floral wire. Wrap the ribbon around, then wind it about 5 times loosely around the ring. Bend half the medium-gauge wire into a U-shaped staple, push it over the posy stems and press the wire ends into the straw wreath. Trim the ends of the ribbon by cutting them on a slant.

Spread a thick layer of glue on the surface of the wreath form, working on a small area at a time. Make sure the glue spreads in between the hollows in the wreath form.

Press the potpourri firmly onto the glue. It is surprising how much will stick. Spread glue on the next area around the form, press on more potpourri, continuing until the form, including the sides, is covered.

SACHETS FOR A DRAWER

Sachets are one of the easiest and most popular ways to use potpourri. They are a simple craft item for a child or a beginning seamstress. And, because you can use scraps of material and lace left over from other projects, they are inexpensive.

YOU WILL NEED

Two 5- × 5- inch squares of fabric of your choice
25 inches lace
Small portion potpourri
Pins
Iron

The fabric sets the tone for the sachet. It can be country calico, a contemporary fabric of bright colors and abstract design, an elegant satin, or a Victorian floral. It can be trimmed with the simplest bit of ribbon or an elaborate length of antique lace. It can be decorated with embroidery or applique, and trimmed with dried flowers.

Sachets are placed in lingerie drawers and linen closets, and hung in clothes closets. If you place writing papers in lingerie drawers, the sachets perfume them, too.

With the lace pinned to the right side of 1 square, pin the 2 squares together, right sides facing. On 1 side, using a hot iron, turn a ½-inch hem along the top.

Stitch along the 3 sides that do not have a hem. Trim the corners and turn right-side out, ironing if needed.

Fill with potpourri. With the hem turned in and the lace pinned in place, stitch the fourth side closed.

HANGING SACHETS

YOU WILL NEED

6- × 8- inch piece of cotton
24 inches narrow ribbon
25 inches lace
Small amount potpourri
Iron

With a hot iron, press under a ½-inch hem along the long edge of the fabric, then stitch the hem down.

Cut the ribbon into two 12-inch pieces. Fold 1 piece in half, making a loop, then stitch both ends of the loop to the hem, on the wrong side of the fabric. Fold the fabric in half sideways, right sides facing, with the hem along the top edge. Stitch bottom and side. Trim the corners, turn right-side out, and iron if needed. Fill about two-thirds of the bag with potpourri. Stitch the bag shut just above the potpourri, and tie with the ribbon.

ROUNDED HANGING SACHETS

YOU WILL NEED

12-inch circle of fabric
30 inches ribbon
Iron
Potpourri

With a hot iron, press under a ¼-inch hem around the edge of the cloth, then stitch. Cut the ribbon into two 15-inch pieces. Fold 1 piece in half, making a loop. Sew both ends of the loop to the wrong side of the fabric, at the edge. Make a row of long running stitches around the circumference of the fabric, about 1 inch from the edge. Leave long tails of thread. Cup the fabric in your hand, wrong side up, and place a mound of potpourri on it. Pull the tails of thread so they gather the neck of the pouch. Tie firmly. Tie the remaining piece of ribbon around the neck, and make a bow.

MOBILE

Each sachet contains only a small amount of potpourri. This mobile is perfect if you wish to perfume a large closet or guest room.

YOU WILL NEED

Two 12-inch pieces of dowel
Ribbon or cord
6 potpourri sachets (see page 73)

Small spray of dried flowers, such as straw-flowers

Form a cross with the pieces of dowel, then tie them firmly with a small piece of ribbon or cord: You can also use a dot of glue to secure them. Decorate the crosspiece with the spray of dried flowers (or simply put some straw-flowers on the cross as I have done).

Tie 2 sachets on a piece of ribbon or cord, so that they hang one above the other, about 12 inches apart. Suspend them from the crosspiece.

Tie each of the remaining 4 sachets at the end of a dowel, preferably so they hang approximately halfway between the height of 2 sachets in the center. If necessary, reinforce with glue so the ribbons do not slip off the end of the mobile.

Alternatively, instead of dowels, use 20 to 30 inches of cord. Tie a small loop at one end of the cord: That end will be the top, and the loop will let you hang it on a hook or hanger. Beginning about 6 inches from the top, loop the cord around the neck of a sachet and tie lightly. Tie the remaining sachets at equal intervals along the piece of the cord.

MINI-BASKET MOBILE

YOU WILL NEED

Tree branch painted white
Vase
Glue sticks and a glue gun
3 baskets, 2 to 3 inches long
Potpourri
Ribbon

Small dried straw-flowers

Place the branch in a vase.

With hot glue, attach the dried straw-flowers round the edge of each basket or elsewhere on the branch.

Then, simply fill the baskets with potpourri, and hang around the branch. To complete the look, tie some ribbon around the base of the branch.

A DIFFERENT KIND OF TEA COSY

Protect your furniture by placing this special sachet under a hot teapot or cup of tea or coffee, so the heat releases the fragrance of potpourri.

YOU WILL NEED

7½- × 7½-inch piece of cotton filling
Two 7½- × 7½-inch pieces of cheesecloth
Potpourri of your choice
8- × 8-inch fabric of your choice
2 strips Velcro
Lace and ribbon, optional

Pin the filling to the wrong side of 1 cheesecloth square. With right sides together, stitch the cheesecloth squares and filler together on 3 sides. Trim the corners, then turn right-side out. Fill loosely with potpourri. The pillow should be squishy, not firm, so a teapot or cup is stable.

To make cloth covers, with right sides facing, stitch the squares of the outer cover along 3 sides. Trim the corners. Affix the Velcro.

Slip outer cover over the potpourri pillow, and close. You can decorate with pieces of lace and ribbon if you like.

BATH SACHETS

Add to the pleasure of soaking in a soothing bath by perfuming the water with potpourri. You can do this by tossing in a "tea bag" of fragrant flowers or herbs. For this purpose, omit the orrisroot and any ground spices that would wash out of the bags, and just use leaves and petals.

YOU WILL NEED

Cheesecloth or loose-weave muslin, cut into circles
Potpourri, see box
Ribbon

Cup the cheesecloth circle in your hand, wrong side up, and place a mound of potpourri on it. Gather together, then tie with some ribbon. Make the ribbon ends long enough so you can make a loop to hang the sachet from the faucet. If you hang the bag so the warm running water runs through it, it will increase the perfume of the water. Then toss the sachet in the bath water.

To give these bath "tea bags" as a gift, pack them in a pretty jar decorated with dried flowers or herbs, attach a ribbon and bow, and tie a sprig of dried flowers into the bow. Or, put them in a basket to which you have glued dried flowers or sprigs of dried herbs, and woven with ribbon. These look attractive displayed with small guest soaps and loose potpourri.

BATH POTPOURRI SUGGESTIONS

1 cup dried rose petals
Pinch dried lavender
1 tbsp grated and dried lemon peel

½ cup dried rosemary spikes
½ cup dried pine needles and tips of branches
Several dried marigolds
Pinch dried thyme

2 tbsp dried lavender
2 tbsp dried chamomile
½ cup dried sage
Pinch dried marjoram

Equal parts dried roses, lilac and carnations.

CHAPTER SIX

pressed flowers

ABOVE *Primulas are considered ideal plant specimens for pressing. Other prime candidates include pansies, leaves, geraniums, and hydrangeas.*

RIGHT *Good mildew-free specimens of carnations, rose petals, and calyxces. "Pressing" flowers in a microwave takes minutes compared with weeks if a wooden press is used.*

If you are a true flower lover, you have probably wished more than once you could frame a breathtakingly lovely bloom that had more natural artistry than any painting or photograph hanging on your wall.

You can do just that through the old-fashioned art of pressing and preserving flowers, but with a modern twist: By drying and "pressing" the flowers and leaves in the microwave oven, you can do in minutes what takes two to eight weeks in a traditional wooden press or between the pages of a heavy book.

Not all flowers retain their color and beauty after being subjected to the twin stresses of pressure and heat, but many do. Those flowers and foliage can be turned into a variety of delightful creations, from greeting cards and framed "picture" arrangements, to placemats and decorations on jewelry boxes.

Pressing flowers by any method is exacting and sometimes frustrating work, and creating a tiny arrangement of the pressed flowers requires a great deal of precision and patience. But the results can be striking.

Begin by surveying your garden – not just the obvious blooms in your flower-beds, but also the leaves and seedheads in your herb garden, the brightly colored autumn leaves on a maple or Chinese pistache tree, the curvy tendrils on weeds, the odd grasses in your lawn.

Anything close to two-dimensional is a prime candidate for pressing. Pansies are perfect, leaves are wonderful, and cinquefoils, anemones, clematis, primulas, geraniums, and hydrangeas are all excellent candidates.

But don't stop there. Thicker flowers like roses, azaleas, chrysanthemums, calendulas, and dahlias can also be "pressed" in the microwave, but require more time and effort. Stalks of flowers like larkspur, baby's-breath, snapdragon, and goldenrod can be left intact and pressed in profile. Daffodils with short trumpets can be pressed successfully if you cut several slits in the trumpet and make the pieces lie flat.

Flowers like carnations and marigolds, which have deep calyxes, can be more difficult. If you cut the calyx off, the flower falls apart, yet if you leave it on, it leaves an ugly bump in the flower's face.

RIGHT The method of pressing leaves in the microwave follows exactly the same principle as for flowers – laying them between 2 plates (see page 80).

LEFT Three-dimensional daffodils with short trumpets can be pressed successfully by slicing it in half and pressing the halves in profile.

Some people advocate taking apart thick flowers, like roses or ones with long calyxes, and drying each petal separately, then reassembling the pieces in the design. This process will quickly frustrate a novice. Instead, begin with simpler flowers and leaves, then if you discover a love and a talent for arranging pressed flowers, try the more complicated flowers. One possible shortcut: Thin the flower by removing and discarding some unnecessary petals.

Not all flowers survive being pressed in a microwave. Once the water is removed from fleshy flowers like orchids and African violets, there is little substance left to work with.

Some flowers lose their color to dehydration. Gardenias turn an ugly brown; the blue washes out of blue marguerites; sweet woodruff goes black; and lithodora, or heavenly blues, turn pink.

The colors that remain truest are purples, greens, yellows, and oranges. Most blues fade, and many reds turn brown or fade to beige. Some whites stay true, but many turn a lovely cream. Autumn leaves usually keep their bright colors, because the change of seasons has already removed much of their moisture naturally.

In selecting flowers for pressing, keep these tips in mind:

- Pick flowers when their surfaces are dry, not wet from dew, rain, or irrigation. Wet flowers dry unevenly.
- The flaws in damaged flowers are magnified by pressing. On the other hand, you can easily remove a damaged petal or two from a rose that has many to spare.
- Pick flowers not quite at full bloom. A flower that has passed its peak is more likely to lose its color during pressing.
- Look for unusual shapes and textures.
- Pick lots of extras, because you will make mistakes.

Try to press only one kind of leaf or flower at a time, but if you cannot, at least avoid pressing two types of flowers that are very different because they take different amounts of time and sometimes different power levels. Most leaves can be pressed together. Chrysanthemums and dahlias are of similar shape, thickness, and delicacy, and can be pressed together. Snapdragons in profile and pansies in full face can be twinned.

PRESSING FLOWERS AND LEAVES IN THE MICROWAVE

YOU WILL NEED

2 microwave-safe plates
2 squares of plain blotting paper, possibly extra
Dish towel or pot-holder
Pair of tweezers

Primula plants
Selection of leaves, such as weeping fig, honesty, ivy, geranium

1 Turn 1 dish upside down, cover with a piece of blotting paper, and arrange some flowers face down or in profile.

SUGGESTED TIMES FOR PRESSING FLOWERS AND LEAVES

Simpler flowers and leaves cook at Medium-Low power (40 percent) for 15 minutes for the most delicate flowers, like geraniums; 20 minutes for some leaves and slightly hardier flowers, like pansies, snapdragons, and baby's-breath; and 25 minutes for thicker or fuzzy leaves, like dusty miller. Thicker flowers, like roses, dahlias, azaleas, stocks and chrysanthemums, are more difficult. They seem to hold their color and shape best if cooked at lower power for longer periods. At Low power (20 percent), they take 35 to 50 minutes.

2 Cover with another piece of blotting paper and the second dish, turned upright.

3 Place in the microwave. Cooking times will vary greatly (see page 80). Check the flowers at 10-minute intervals and straighten any petals that are inadvertantly turned or twisted. If the paper under them is wet, carefully pick them up with a pair of tweezers and move them to a drier section. Be very careful as the flowers tear easily when they are limp and wet, and snap off when they are dry and brittle. At this stage put extra weight on the thicker flowers if necessary. Replace top blotting paper and plate, and return to microwave until brittle or stiff.

4 Remove flowers with extreme care, and set aside to cool. They may be stored flat, between sheets of paper.

DESIGNING AN ARRANGEMENT

Just as you look for balance and proportion in a three-dimensional flower arrangement, you must look for the same qualities in two-dimensional arrangements. The focal point of an arrangement does not have to be dead center – in fact, it is often more attractive if it is off center – but the lines created by your design should converge naturally at the focal point.

Do not create a lopsided arrangement, with all the flowers crowded into one area and an awkward amount of space left empty. That does not mean you cannot decorate the corner of a card with a border of flowers: Borders create lines that naturally carry the eye to the center and frame whatever is there, such as a written message.

Do not crowd too many flowers into a single arrangement. The white space between flowers helps delineate individual blossoms and sets off their shape: A great mass of flowers just creates a busy jumble. Simple designs are among the prettiest.

Begin at the focal point and work your way out. The largest blossoms and leaves should be at the focal point, graduating to smaller flowers and leaves at the edges.

You can overlap and overlay flowers. A line of small red or yellow flowers, for example, overlaying a chain of large green leaves creates a flowing and natural looking line giving it continuity.

In addition to the projects described below, you can use the same basic designs to decorate many objects: Placemats, boxes, flat-sided jars, bookmarks, napkin holders, and spice racks are just a few ideas for you to try.

MECHANICS OF ARRANGING PRESSED FLOWERS

- *Because pressed flowers are so delicate, plan your design first on a piece of paper, to cut down on amount of handling, THEN apply glue.*
- *Always work somewhere draft free and not near an open window.*
- *Leave thick margins around the edges, so you don't inadvertantly cover part of your design with the frame.*
- *Don't use a hot glue gun. The beads of glue begin to harden immediately, and form ugly bumps in the flower face.*
- *Put a small amount of glue in a dish, and use a toothpick to apply tiny dots of adhesive.*
- *Protect your design. Use a glass pane for a framed arrangement; protective film on cards, placemats, and bookmarks; and a clear lacquer or other glaze on flowers mounted on wood.*

BOOKMARKS

The role of the bookmark is a perfect one for a pressed flower design; for if it is used for its intended purpose, it remains flat within a protective book. This is a good project for beginners or children.

YOU WILL NEED

Thin cardboard
Extra plain paper
Toothpicks
Glue
Small, soft brush
Spray fixative, optional

Selection of pressed flowers, such as astrantias, buttercups, pansies
Selection of pressed foliage, such as Queen Anne's lace, small leaves

Cut the cardboard to a suitable shape: If you have a means of cutting an attractive deckled edge, or if you are able to outline the cardboard, so much the better, but this is not essential.

Make sure the cardboard is dry and dust-free. Plan the picture on a piece of paper beforehand and make it up in a place where there are no drafts or open windows.

Dip a toothpick into the glue and lightly touch the back of each petal and manoevre into place with the tip of a small, soft brush. The sticking stage is an important one for unprotected designs so it is necessary to use more than just a single spot. Several tiny spots should be applied to the back of each item, which should then be carefully and firmly smoothed down. The flowers can be invisibly sealed and protected from the moisture by spraying with a spray fixative.

FLOWER CANDLES

Candles adorned with flowers look lovely enough to be used as ornaments and not merely to be burned down and the design destroyed.

YOU WILL NEED

Candles of different sizes and shapes
Varnish
Fine paintbrush
Toothpick

Selection of pressed flowers and foliage, such as daisies, aquilegia, fall leaves

Make sure that the candles are smooth, clean, and dust-free.

Plan the design by placing the flowers onto the candles in the positions they will eventually take. Transfer this design to a temporary surface and apply the first, thin coat of varnish to the candles. Then, while the varnish is still wet, position the flowers in it. If you have placed a flower in the wrong place, or you would like to alter the design, use a toothpick to move the flowers around until they are perfectly positioned. You can move flowers around for about 15 minutes.

When the design is completed, leave it to dry for at least 8 hours in a dust-free place. Apply a second coat of the varnish.

GREETING CARDS

Greeting cards decorated with pressed flowers add a very personal touch to the card on its own or with a gift.

YOU WILL NEED

High-quality construction paper
Scissors, razor blade, or craft knife
Ruler
Pencil
Glue
Self-adhesive film

Selection of pressed flowers and foliage, such as purple and yellow pansies, buttercups, ferns, larkspur, hydrangeas

Cut out a 7- × 10-inch piece of construction paper, using scissors, razor blade, or craft knife held against a ruler. Fold the paper in half, so the card has a 5- × 7-inch face.

Lightly sketch the outline of the design in pencil on the face of the card, then use it as your guide for attaching the flowers and foliage.

Find the center point of the card: It can be horizontal or vertical. Arrange the foliage in 5 spokes radiating out from the center: They do not need to meet at the center. Attach the biggest flower (pansy or buttercup) over the centerpoint. Scatter some smaller flowers around the main flower and between the spokes, but do not glue them to the card. Use bits of foliage for curving stems that point to, but don't reach, the pansy. Glue the stems, then the smaller flowers over their ends.

Carefully cover the design with self-adhesive film so it is well protected. If not placed down properly, there may be bubbles, so practise on designs that do not matter or you will be very disappointed if a lovely piece of work is ruined by the faulty film.

DAISY AND PRIMULA RING

This pretty ring can be framed and hung on a wall to be admired permanently, or even made into a placemat by placing it on a cork mat and covering it in heat-resistant material.

YOU WILL NEED

Thick cardboard
Scissors
Glue
Ribbon, optional

Selection of pressed daisies, primulas

Cut out a ring from the cardboard (you can use a plate or saucer as a template if necessary).

Spread glue over small sections of the cardboard.

Arrange the flowers in concentric circles starting with the daisies on the outside and working in toward the center. Continue working in sections until the whole thing is covered. If you wish, you can top the ring with a bow tied of narrow ribbon in a toning color.

CHAPTER SEVEN

clay and dough

Imagine a Christmas tree, covered with handmade decorations, or a brighly colored centerpiece for your table, also made by hand. Imagine pretty jewelry or abstractly shaped paperweights that look deceptively like expensive folk art. These are a long way from the ugly clay ashtrays often made during the first years of school – our first work of sculpture, personalized with our hand print, painted a hideous shade of green, and proudly presented to our parents. Yet, these pretty artistic creations are just as easy to make as those awful ashtrays.

You do not need special equipment, a lot of time, or exceptional artistic skill to make these projects. The processes described in this chapter are so easy and inexpensive you will be comfortable experimenting, even if you discard many of your first creations. For the same reasons, making clay-like objects is a perfect activity for children, who can pummel and shape their creations, then paint them wild colors.

With the microwave oven, you do not have to wait 24 hours or longer for your creation to air-dry and be ready for paint. Small flat ornaments can be dried in as little as 5 minutes, while larger objects take longer: Any of the projects in this chapter can be completed in an afternoon. They are sure to inspire your own ideas for creations.

Use tempura, acrylic paint, or food coloring, although the latter may fade with time. Mix the coloring into the dough before baking, especially if you're making a single-color item, like a red heart. Or, divide the plain dough into several parts, color each separately, then shape your creation with colored doughs: You can touch up the colors after the item is baked. But be forewarned: Coloring the raw dough is a messy process. And be careful about using rolling pins, bread boards, and other kitchen tools that come into contact with food. You may want to paint the finished item with a lacquer or other sealant to improve the finish, as well as protect it against insects or humidity.

ABOVE *Drying dough projects in the microwave such as this dough dolly, means you do not have to wait 24 hours or longer to paint your design. (By courtesy of Vesutor Ltd., Sussex, England.)*

RIGHT *Although these dough bread rings look good enough to eat, they are inedible and to be used for decoration (see page 96).*

This chapter has three recipes for clay-like substances to shape and bake in a microwave oven. All are simple and safe, and will keep, uncooked, for several days in your refrigerator. One uses only stale bread and white glue, the second is a mixture of flour, salt, and water, the third is made with cornstarch, baking soda, and water. The projects that follow can be made with any of the recipes, although each has special properties.

Any clay or dough items may scorch in the microwave, especially thicker items that must cook for a long time. The greatest danger is whenever dough comes into contact with another surface. The dough and the dish or microwave rack build up heat between them, which can cause an ugly brown scorchmark. The Bread-and-Glue Dough (page 92) is especially susceptible to this. However, if you plan to

paint the item after baking, no harm is done.

The Flour-and-Salt Clay should be used within a few days of making. You must lightly wet the surface of unbaked pieces if they are to stick together. The surface tends to show evidence of joints and patches more readily than the bread-and-glue mix, and thick objects tend to develop surface cracks in the microwave. Even fully dried items may have problems in humid climates, because the salt causes the clay to absorb moisture, so some items soften. Avoid this problem by sealing the object with a varnish or other substance. Although you can mix paint or other coloring into the dough before baking, the salt rises to the surface and leaves a white, powdery residue that often needs to be touched up. On the other hand, this mixture is less expensive than the bread-glue mix and is not as likely to be troubled by hungry insects.

The Bread-and-Glue Dough tends to get a little puffier when heated than the Flour-and-Salt Clay. The items may also shrink in size. You may find the bread-glue dough more rubbery and easier to handle, unbaked pieces adhere to each other without wetting the surfaces, and thick items are not as likely to crack. It is easier to mix coloring into the dough before baking – a definite plus if you are a clumsy painter. You can create a ceramic-like finish by painting the surface with a mixture of equal parts of water and white glue, but don't apply that mixture until halfway through the baking if you've made detailed impressions in the surface. Insects are attracted to items made with the bread-glue mix, a problem that can be forestalled by lacquering the item or – if there are no children in the house who are likely to eat anything that resembles a cookie – mixing in a little borax or crushed mothballs. This mixture is more expensive than the flour and salt, but the unbaked bread-glue mixture keeps longer in the refrigerator.

The cornstarch and baking soda mixture can be more difficult to work with than either of the other recipes because it tends to be more fragile. It does not, however, shrink or puff like the bread-glue mix, it has a fine-grained texture, and stays whiter than the others. It needs to be microwaved as part of the mixing process. It does not keep well unbaked. It is very absorbent and requires more coats of paint and glaze than the other mixes.

If you're a clumsy painter, I strongly recommend that you divide the uncooked dough into parts, and color each part before baking, as I have done in the Autumn Wreath project. You can touch it up after baking, especially if you're working with the flour-salt clay. But you can easily ruin a simple snowman by trying to paint black buttons onto the white surface.

FLOUR-AND-SALT CLAY

Although this project makes cookie shapes, the basic ingredients and method can be used for any of the projects featured in this book.

YOU WILL NEED

4 cups flour, plus extra for rolling
1 cup salt
Wooden spoon
1½ cups water
Paint (optional)
Pastry board
Rolling pin
Cookie cutters
Vegetable oil
Pastry brush
Microwave-safe plate

1 Mix the flour and salt together, then stir in 1 cup water.

2 Knead the clay well. Add the remaining water to the clay as needed and knead until smooth and pliable. If you add paint or other liquid coloring, you may need to work in a little extra flour to thicken the clay. Roll out the clay on a board.

3 Then cut out shapes with cookie cutters. You can also cut your own designs using cardboard or stiff paper as templates.

4 Place the items on a lightly oiled microwave-safe plate or other flat dish. Bake at Medium Power (50 percent) for about 12 minutes, checking at 2-minute intervals, until the surfaces are hard. Watch carefully, as items scorch quickly if they cook too long. It is better to err on the side of too little baking time, since the clay or dough can finish drying in the open air.

5 After microwaved items have sat for about 15 minutes and are completely dry, they are ready to be decorated. You can make a variety of items with these flat "cookies." Put a smaller item on a chain and create a necklace; glue a small magnet to the back after baking, and use it as a refrigerator magnet; and to make a Christmas tree ornament, see below.

LEARN TO BE CREATIVE

If you want to use any of the basic cookie shapes as Christmas ornaments or a pendant to hang on a chain, use a toothpick to poke a hole at the top of the item before baking. You can also use a toothpick, end of a straw, and other items to make a pattern of impressions in the surface. Make the impressions deeper in the Flour-and-Salt Clay than if you are working with the Bread-and-Glue Dough or the Cornstarch Dough (see page 92).

BREAD-AND-GLUE DOUGH

Stale bread is a good choice for this mixture. If you use fresh bread, let it sit out for an hour or two so it dries out a little.

YOU WILL NEED

10 slices of white bread
10 tbsp white glue

Cut the crusts off the bread and discard or save them for making bread crumbs: Brown crusts tend to leave brown spots in the dough mix.

Using a medium bowl, tear the bread into small pieces and add the first 8 tablespoons of glue. Mix and knead with your hands: It is a very stickly and unwieldy mixture at first, but it becomes smooth as you work with it. Once it becomes smooth, add additional glue if it is too stiff to work easily.

Later, as you work with the dough, you can thin it with water or thicken it with white flour.

CORNSTARCH DOUGH

YOU WILL NEED

3 cups baking soda
$1\frac{1}{2}$ cups cornstarch
$2\frac{3}{4}$ cups water

Combine all the ingredients in a microwave-safe board and stir well. Cook at Medium Power (50 percent), stirring at 3-minute intervals, until thick and difficult to stir. Let it stand, covered with a damp towel, until it is cool enough to handle. Knead thoroughly.

BREAD BASKET

YOU WILL NEED

$\frac{1}{2}$ batch Flour-and-Salt Clay, see page 90
Pastry board
Microwave-safe bowl
Vegetable oil for bowl
Milk or mayonnaise for glaze

Roll out uncolored clay to the thickness of a pie crust. Cut the dough into strips about $\frac{3}{4}$-inches wide. Choose a microwave-safe bowl the same size as you want the finished basket to be. Turn it upside down and lightly oil the outside.

Lay 2 parallel strips across the center of the bowl, about $\frac{1}{2}$ inch apart. Take another strip, lay it across the center of the 2 strips at a right angle, then weave it under one of the strips to begin a lattice work. Especially if you are working with the Flour-and-Salt Clay, it is important to moisten all the surfaces that are supposed to adhere to another strip. By the time you have worked your way up the basket sides, you will be patching strips together, and the joints need to be secure.

Bake the bowl and basket at Medium power (50 percent). Check the basket at 3-minute intervals. When the dough has begun to harden, gently loosen it from the bowl, but leave it on the bowl and cook for a few more minutes. When the basket can hold its own shape without the bowl, remove the bowl. You can glaze the bowl with milk or mayonnaise thinned with a little water, which browns like bread. Continue baking until the basket is firm. Leave to cool. Line with a pretty napkin.

SNOWMAN

This snowman is simple to make, but because of the thickness of the item and the danger of scorching, you should do only part of the drying in the microwave. The flour-and-salt mixture is likely to crack with an item this thick. The bread-glue mixture is a better choice.

YOU WILL NEED

1 batch Bread-and-Glue Dough, see page 92
Black paint
Rolling pin
Pastry board
Round cookie cutter
Vegetable oil for plate
Microwave-safe plate

Roll out 3 balls of dough, each successively smaller. Beginning with the largest ball, place 1 on top of the other. Color about one-third of the dough black.

Roll out a small amount of dough as you would a cookie, and cut out a circle, approximately the same diameter as the largest ball: This will be the brim of the snowman's hat. If you tried to use it raw, it would sag. Instead, bake it about 2 minutes, just until it starts to hold its shape. Place on top of the snowman's head. Roll out a short cylinder of dough to make the rest of the snowman's top hat. Place on top of the brim. You can give the snowman extra support by running a wooden skewer through the length of his body, but it is not necessary.

Roll out tiny balls of dough to create his eyes, nose, and mouth, and his buttons. Wetting the dough slightly, attach each to the body in the appropriate position.

Set the snowman on a lightly oiled microwave-safe plate. Bake for 10 minutes at Medium power (50 percent). Remove the snowman from the plate and leave both to cool a little, then bake again, checking at 6 to 8 minute intervals. Make sure the bottom doesn't scorch. You can either let the snowman cool between the cooking periods, or let it finish drying in the air rather than the microwave.

AUTUMN WREATH

You can hang this wreath on a wall, but it also makes an attractive centerpiece.

YOU WILL NEED

Selection of garden leaves
Pencil
Cardboard or stiff paper
Scissors
2 batches Bread-and-Glue Dough, see page 92
3 paints of complementary colors
Waxed paper
Pastry board
Rolling pin
Knife
Microwave-safe plate
Vegetable oil for plate
Glue sticks and a glue gun

Choose a variety of leaves from your garden, the more varied the shapes, the better. Trace their outlines onto cardboard or stiff paper, and cut out the shapes.

Divide 1 batch of dough for leaves into at least 3 sections, and knead a different color paint – such as scarlet, orange, and gold – into each.

Roll out the first color of dough between 2 pieces of waxed paper. Using the cardboard templates, cut the leaf shapes from the dough. Use the point of a knife to create a serrated edge, and lightly trace some veins.

Place the leaves on a lightly oiled, microwave-safe platter, and bake at Medium power (50 percent), checking at 2-minute intervals, until firm, 10 to 15 minutes, depending on thickness. Leave leaves to cool while you work on the wreath.

Meanwhile, to make the wreath, work brown paint into the second batch of dough. On a flat surface, roll dough into a cylinder, rolling and stretching into a rope about 1-inch thick. Make into a ring, and seal the ends. Use a knife to make deep, horizontal cuts, resembling branches or twigs.

Place the wreath on a lightly oiled plate, and bake at Medium power (50 percent). Check at 5-minute intervals. When the wreath is stiff enough to hold its own shape, turn it over and continue baking. It should take at least 30 minutes. When it is firm, remove, and leave to cool.

Arrange the leaves around the inside and outside of the ring, varying shapes and colors. Use hot glue and a glue gun to attach the leaves to the wreath.

BOWL

This bowl is conducive to creative decorating, and can be used for fruit or as a vase.

YOU WILL NEED

Microwave-safe bowl
Vegetable oil for bowl
¾ batch Flour-and-Salt Clay, see page 90
Paint or coloring of your choice
Clear lacquer

Choose a microwave-safe bowl the same size and shape that you want the finished product to be. Turn it upside down and lightly oil the outside.

If you choose, you can work paint or other coloring into the clay at this point. Then take a fistful of clay and roll it between your hands to form a short, stubby cylinder with a smooth surface. Place it on a flat surface, and roll it with your hands, applying pressure and stretching it until it forms a long, skinny rope, ¼-inch to ½-inch thick.

Beginning at table level, wrap the rope around the edge of the bowl, then gradually work up the sides of the bowl. As you cover the bowl's base, make a coil of the rope: You will need several ropes to complete the bowl. Use water to make sure the joints are secure and smooth, and to seal each row to the one it sits on.

Bake the bowl and the rope basket at Medium power (50 percent), checking at 10-minute intervals. When the basket begins to harden, gently loosen it from the bowl and continue baking. When it is stiff enough to hold its own shape, remove it from the bowl and continue baking.

Because this bowl is so thick, it takes a long time to bake and will get quite hot: The heat from the clay may scorch a plastic bowl or melt it slightly. The clay also may scorch if it comes into contact with an oven rack for long periods. You may want to leave the bowl to finish by air-drying.

When the bowl is cool, paint it, then seal it with clear lacquer or other finish. Never put water into the bowl as it will cause the dough to soften.

SMALL DOUGH RINGS

These attractive dough rings are deceptive; in fact, they are very simple to make.

YOU WILL NEED

2 batches Flour-and-Salt Clay, see page 90
Water
Cherries and currants, optional
1 egg yolk, beaten
Paper towel
Microwave-safe plate
Candles, optional

Make a dough ring from 1 batch of dough, by rolling out a thick sausage and joining the ends together. Dampen the ring with a little water.

The dough rings can be decorated in many different ways. Here are some ideas for you to try: Strips of dough placed like petals over the base ring (see top ring in picture); coils of dough making up seven rings with an optional cherry placed in the center of each (see right ring in picture); and alternating strips and balls of dough (see left ring in picture). Glaze rings with egg yolk.

Place some paper towels on the plate, place ring on top and bake for about 20 minutes on Medium power (50 percent) checking halfway. Leave to cool.

LARGE DOUGH RING

This makes a very attractive table centerpiece.

YOU WILL NEED

3 batches Flour-and-Salt Clay, see page 90
1 egg yolk, beaten
Paper towels
Microwave-safe plate

Begin by making a very large dough ring (see above for instructions) with 1 batch of dough. Make a long 3-strand braid from the second batch of dough and position around the outside of the ring. Then, small dough balls should make 2 rings inside the braid. Roll out the remaining dough and cut out four leaves; the leaves should then be stuck onto the braid.

Glaze the ring with beaten egg yolk. Place some paper towel on a microwave-safe plate and bake for about 30 minutes on Medium power (50 per cent), checking at 10 minute intervals. Leave to cool.

CHAPTER EIGHT

papier-mâché

Papier-mâché is messy, fun, and inexpensive. Strips of wet, gluey paper or globs of wet, gluey pulp are stuck to an inflated balloon or ball of chicken wire until a recognizable form emerges. When the paper or pulp dries and hardens, the item is painted and glazed, resulting in a rigid, light-weight creation of molded paper.

The primary ingredients are newspaper, flour, water, paint, clear glaze, and whatever items are needed to give features to the creation, such as yarn for the hair of a papier-mâché doll.

Traditionally, papier-mâché is made without heat. Using a microwave, however, speeds the process. It also gives a better sense of the emerging shape of the messy, dripping form in front of you. There are two specific advantages when you use the microwave partially to dry a form at intervals as you build up its shape. First, the slippery strips of paper begin to harden in place and stop sliding around, and, second, it is easier to see dimples and bumps on a dry surface.

ABOVE A papier-mâché plate can be made using the layering method such as this one, or the pulp method (see page 100).

To use the microwave, however, you cannot use a balloon or chicken wire as your form. Instead, use tightly wadded newspaper, paper tubes from inside a roll of wrapping paper, or cardboard boxes. Everything can be bundled together with tape for a microwave-safe base.

Two papier-mâché techniques are popular. The pulp method uses pulp made from disintegrated newspaper, and the layering method uses strips of paper. Both types can be combined in one project.

For both types, you will need a large quantity of newspaper, torn into 1-inch strips.

MAKING PULP IN THE MICROWAVE

This method requires some advance preparation, preferably at least four to six hours before you begin. The paper needs to stew in hot water to speed its deterioration into pulp.

YOU WILL NEED

Shredded paper or newspaper
1 quart boiling water
Microwave-safe bowl
Wooden spoon
Colander or wire strainer
1 cup P.V.A. (and/or wallpaper paste containing fungicide) or paste of 1 cup flour and 1 cup water

1 To make the pulp, take shredded paper or tear strips of newspaper into 1-inch strips. Put them in a microwave-safe bowl with a 2- to 3-quart capacity, until almost full of paper bits. At the same time, bring 1 quart of water to a boil in the microwave. Slowly pour the boiling water into the bowl with the newspaper, stirring continuously. When the paper is soaked, it should be just covered with water. If more water is needed to cover the paper, use warm tap water.

2 Put the bowl in the microwave and cook on High power (100 percent) for 10 minutes. Remove it from the oven, stir well, and leave it to stand. You should see the paper starting to disintegrate. Return the pulp to the microwave every hour for 10 minutes, then stir and leave to stand again. The pulp will be usable after 4 to 6 hours, but it can stand up to 24 hours.

3 Using a colander or wire strainer, drain the pulp. Squeeze out most but not all of the remaining water.

4 Thoroughly mix in the P.V.A. Sprinkle in enough dry wallpaper paste to give the pulp a workable consistency, mixing it quickly. An alternative method is to make a paste of 1 cup flour and 1 cup water. It should be soupy, so adjust amounts if necessary. For every cup of pulp, mix in ⅓ cup of paste, until it forms a thick mush.

5 The pulp is now ready for use. Store it in a plastic bag in the refrigerator or use immediately.

DECORATIVE PLATE

This project and the next one have been left undecorated but if you are feeling creative, take out your paints and have some fun.

YOU WILL NEED

2 microwave-safe plates, one larger than the other
Plastic wrap
1 batch pulp, see page 99
Metal spoon
Vegetable oil for plate
Gesso or a mix of P.V.A. and acrylic paint
Paintbrush

Line the top of the plate mold with plastic wrap. Then press pulp evenly onto the inside of the plate mold to a thickness of $\frac{1}{4}$ to $\frac{1}{2}$ inch. Leave to dry slightly. Smooth the surface of the pulp with the back of a large metal spoon.

Decorate the rim with more pulp, then place on an oiled plate and dry in the microwave for about 5 minutes on Medium power (50 percent). The surface of the plate should now be dry. Carefully remove the pulp plate from the mold and allow the plate to dry completely. Finish the underside by making a foot-rim with more pulp. When the pulp is completely dry, seal it with a coat of Gesso or a 1:3 mixture of P.V.A. and acrylic paint.

TRAY

This project is based on using more cardboard and less pulp, allowing more even and faster drying.

YOU WILL NEED

Craft knife
Polyboard, corrugated cardboard, or mounting cardboard
P.V.A.
Staples
Tape
Newspaper
Glue
1 batch pulp, see page 99
Brush
Textured wallpaper or felt, optional
Clear varnish

Cut out all the shapes needed for the base and handles of the tray. To make a strong enough base, use polyboard or laminate several layers of cardboard held together with P.V.A. Attach handles firmly to the base, using staples, tape, and any other means to ensure a solid structure. The cardboard structure gives the piece its strength – not the pulp – so it is important to attach the handles very firmly before the pulp is added.

Build up the rim by scrunching up bits of newspaper, then gluing and taping into place. Smooth the paper down as much as possible. Brush on P.V.A. Take some of the pulp and mold it firmly into place over rim and handles of the tray.

Decorate the rim with some molded pulp (see finished project). Leave to dry slightly until the pulp is firm.

Turn the tray over and add more pulp to the underside of the rim and handles to strengthen them. If necessary, neaten the underside of the tray by gluing on a backing, such as textured wallpaper or felt. When the tray is completely dry, brush on a coat of Gesso to seal the surface. The tray is now ready for further decorating, if wished.

EARRINGS

These bright flower earrings look very attractive and although they are very large, they are very light. In this project, the microwave is part of the method.

YOU WILL NEED

Pencil
Thin cardboard, 4 × 4 inches
Craft knife or scissors
Wallpaper paste
Wire cooling rack
Paper
Fine sandpaper
White emulsion paint
Poster paints
Black ink
Clear varnish
Darning needle
P.V.A.
2 pairs earring hooks and eyes
Strong, clear glue
1 pair clip fastenings
Small pair pliers

Draw the earring shapes onto thin cardboard.

Cut around the shapes with a craft knife or scissors. Paint the cut-out shapes with 1 coat watered-down P.V.A. adhesive. Allow the earrings partially to dry in the microwave for 3–4 minutes on Medium power (50 percent), then leave the earrings on a cooling rack for about 2 hours to dry completely.

Using small strips of paper, about ½ inch × 2 inches, cover the earring shapes with 3 layers of pasted paper. Work carefully around each petal, making sure the papier-mâché does not become too lumpy so it has a smooth finish. Lay papered shapes on a cooling rack to dry for 24 hours.

When the shapes are completely dry, smooth them down lightly with fine sandpaper and coat them with layers of white emulsion paint, allowing first coat to dry before adding second.

Draw the center of the daisy on flower shapes. The petal outlines and swirls are drawn freehand on top of the poster paint with black Indian ink, so there is no need to draw these on the earrings now.

Start filling in the color. The petals are light blue, and then, when this coat dries, paint again with violet, letting the light blue show through in patches. Give the disks 2 coats of yellow paint. Leave to dry for 4 hours.

Using a fine paintbrush, carefully draw in the black outlines and swirls. Let the earrings dry overnight, then varnish the fronts with clear gloss varnish. Lay (varnished side up!) on a wire cooling rack to dry. Varnish the backs and allow them to dry again. Repeat the process so fronts and backs have 2 coats of varnish. Clean brush thoroughly after each coat.

When the second coat of varnish is dry, make a small hole with a darning needle in the top of the petal section and in the bottom of the disk.

Dab a little undiluted P.V.A. adhesive into the holes. Take the earring hook and eyes and push a hook section into the hole in each flower and an eye into each disk.

Dab some strong, clear glue on to earring clips and position 1 on back of each disk. Press the disk and clip together firmly and leave all the earring pieces to dry overnight.

Loop the hook into the eye, joining the disk and the flower, and close the opening with a small pair of pliers. Your earrings are now ready to wear!

CHAPTER NINE

bath and beauty

INGREDIENTS

Here are notes on ingredients, which may aid you in modifying the recipes to suit your own skin type. ALOE GEL is the soothing, jelly-like substance that oozes from the broken leaf of an aloe plant. BEESWAX is an emulsifier, binding and thickening ingredients in a cosmetic cream. It softens and protects the skin. CASTILE SOAP is a soap made from at least 40 percent olive oil. COCOA BUTTER thickens a cosmetic cream, softens, and lubricates the skin. ESSENTIAL OIL is an oil extracted from flowers or herbs, or an oil perfumed with flowers or herbs. It is a pleasing, but – despite its name – not an essential ingredient. GLYCERIN, typically a petroleum by-product, helps soothe and soften skin and preserve its natural moisture. LANOLIN is an emulsifier obtained from the wool of sheep. It helps relieve dry skin. OATMEAL is a mild abrasive agent. ROSE WATER is water in which roses have been steeped for many days, used to close pores and soothe skin. SWEET ALMOND OIL is a pleasant smelling oil used as a base for many homemade cosmetics. Less-expensive olive oil or corn oil can be substituted. WHEAT GERM OIL is a moisturizer and a source of Vitamin E.

Finally, a caution about dishes. The beeswax used in some of these recipes may leave residues that are difficult to clean out of the containers. I strongly recommend against using the same containers for making cosmetics and food.

What did we do before moisturizing creams and potions of unpronounceable ingredients became available at $50 an ounce? The price of some cosmetics is stunningly high. The products in this chapter may not cover all your beauty needs, but they will go far in cutting your cosmetics budget. As a plus, you'll know every ingredient they contain.

All of the ingredients listed here can be purchased in health-food stores, although not every item is available in every store. Some ingredients, such as roses, rosemary, lemons, and lavender, can be grown easily in your backyard.

A note of caution. Just as some of the products at the department store cosmetics' counter will not work for you – and some may even be harmful to your particular hair or skin type – not every concoction in this book is beneficial to everyone. Use these products sparingly until you are comfortable with them.

ROSE WATER AND SPICED WATER

If you have hard water in your area, consider using bottled water for this recipe, which is a delightful way to refresh your face.

YOU WILL NEED

1 cup dried rose petals
or
2 tbsp whole cloves
6 pieces cinnamon, 2-inches long
microwave-safe dish
1 quart water

Place 1 cup of dried rose petals in a microwave-safe dish. Add 1 quart of water. Bring to a boil in the microwave on High power (100 percent). Leave to sit until the water cools, allowing the rose petals to steep in the water. Drain off and save the water, discarding the rose petals. Splash the rose-scented water on your face.

As an alternative, put 2 tablespoons whole cloves and several 2-inch pieces of cinnamon stick in the water instead of the rose petals.

BATH VINEGAR

This simple herbed vinegar brings a pleasant scent to your bath water. Experiment with herbs from your garden. Some suggested combinations: Lavender and chamomile; or rosemary, thyme, and mint.

YOU WILL NEED

2 cups dried herbs
1 quart white-wine vinegar
Microwave-safe bowl

Place the dried herbs in a microwave-safe dish. Pour the vinegar over the herbs, and place in the microwave. Bring to a boil on High power (100 percent). Remove and leave to cool. Pour herbs and vinegar into a jar, then leave to steep for 2 weeks, shaking once daily. Strain the herbs and add the vinegar to your bath.

ROSE TALC

Real roses, reinforced by rose oil, add a lovely scent to this bath powder. You can experiment with other scented flowers and oils, too – perhaps lavender, lilac, or carnation.

YOU WILL NEED

6 ounces unscented talc
2 ounces dried rose petals
Few drops rose oil

Crush and crumble the dried rose petals or run them through a blender until they are tiny bits.

Add 3 to 6 drops of rose oil to the talc, blending with your fingers until well mixed. Add the bits of rose petals, mix well. Leave to sit for at least 1 week.

ROSE COLD CREAM

Many people like the smell of sweet almond oil, but it is expensive and sometimes difficult to find. You can substitute olive or safflower oil for all or part of the almond oil. Use this cold cream to remove dirt and makeup.

YOU WILL NEED

½ cup sweet almond oil
½ ounce beeswax
¼ cup rosewater
Few drops rose oil, optional

Put the oil and beeswax into a small, microwave-safe dish. Microwave on High power (100 percent) until beeswax melts, 4 to 5 minutes. With an eggbeater or electric mixer, beat in the rosewater and rose oil, if desired, until the mixture is creamy. Keep in an airtight container until it is ready for use.

ABOVE The beauty products shown here are from top left: Moisturizer, moisturizing cream, rose cold cream, and cleansing cream with aloe vera.

CLEANSING CREAM WITH ALOE VERA

The olive oil steeps with rosemary for 24 hours, adding a pleasant scent to this cream. Aloe vera gel gives it a soothing feel.

YOU WILL NEED

6 tbsp olive or safflower oil
2 tbsp dried rosemary
2 tbsp lard
1 ounce beeswax
3 tbsp aloe vera gel

Put the oil and rosemary in a microwave-safe bowl. Heat for 5 minutes on High power (100 percent). Leave the oil and rosemary to sit for 24 hours.

Strain the oil and discard the rosemary. Add the lard and beeswax to the rosemary-scented oil, and heat on High until the lard and beeswax melt, 4 to 5 minutes. Stir in the aloe vera gel. Beat until the mixture is smooth and creamy.

MOISTURIZER

You may use sweet almond oil, but the cocoa butter will overpower the smell. Olive or safflower oil will work just as well in this facial moisturizer.

YOU WILL NEED

10 tbsp oil, see above
½ ounce cocoa butter
1 ounce beeswax
½ tbsp lanolin
½ cup rosewater

Put the oil, cocoa butter, and beeswax in microwave-safe dish. Microwave on High power (100 percent) until the beeswax melts, 4 to 5 minutes. Stir in the lanolin. Add the rosewater and beat until mixture is smooth and creamy.

MOISTURIZING CREAM

The vitamin E in the wheat germ oil helps preserve the skin's youthful appearance.

YOU WILL NEED

¼ cup wheat germ oil
1 ounce cocoa butter
½ ounce beeswax
2 tbsp lanolin
2 tbsp glycerin
½ cup rosewater
5–10 drops rose oil, optional

Put the wheat germ oil, cocoa butter, and beeswax in a microwave-safe dish. Microwave on High power (100 percent) until the beeswax and cocoa butter melt, 4 to 5 minutes. Stir in the lanolin and glycerin. With an eggbeater or electric mixer, beat in the rosewater and rose oil, if desired, until mixture is smooth and creamy.

OATMEAL SOAP

Save slivers of soap for this project, or grate a bar of Castile soap. The oatmeal is good for scrubbing your skin.

YOU WILL NEED

3-4 tbsp finely ground oatmeal, uncooked
3-4 ounces soap, in slivers or grated
4-5 tbsp water

Run the oatmeal through a food processor, if necessary, to grind it. The oatmeal should be measured after it is ground.

Place the soap and water in a large microwave-safe dish. Microwave on High power (100 percent) for 2 to 3 minutes, until the soap dissolves: You may need to stir it once or twice. Be careful the hot soap does not foam over the edge of the bowl. Stir in the oatmeal.

Pour the mixture into molds. For larger quantities, pour the soap mixture into a tin can from which you have cut both ends. When it is nearly hard, slice oatmeal soap into bars.

INDEX

Page numbers in *italics* refer to captions to the illustrations